DELICIOUS MAINE DESSERTS

96 Recipes from Easy to Elaborate

Cynthia Finnemore Simonds

Down East

Photography credits:
Pages 35, 39, 42, 45, 46, 50, 52, 55, 58, 62, 63, 88, and front cover, photographs by Randall Smith,
ProPix Professional Imaging.
Pages 9, 10, 14, 17, 22, 24, 28, 30, 31, 32, 36, 40, 65, 68, 71, 73, 74, 77, 78, 79, 80, 82, 87, 89, 93, 95,
96, 97, 99, 100, and 101, photographs by Joseph Corrado, JC Design.
Page 18 photograph by ©Gabrieldome Fotolia.com

ISBN: 978-0-89272-773-5

Library of Congress Cataloging-in-Publication Data

Simonds, Cynthia Finnemore, 1966-
Delicious Maine desserts : 96 recipes from easy to elegant / by Cynthia Finnemore Simonds.
        p. cm.
Includes index.
ISBN 978-0-89272-773-5 (pbk. : alk. paper)
1. Desserts. 2. Cookery–Maine. I. Title.
TX773.S524 2009
641.8'6–dc22
                                2009014034
Design by Lynda Chilton
Printed in China

FCI   5   4   3   2   1

BOOKS·MAGAZINE·ONLINE
www.downeast.com
Distributed to the trade by National Book Network

To all of the people who inspire me.
Your kindness and faith allow me to continually
dwell in possibility.

I would like to recognize three special people: Julia Child, for her joie de vivre in the kitchen; Fred Rogers, for his kindness and belief in the goodness in everyone; and Bill Bonyun, for his inspiration. They instilled much joy in my young heart.

Many thanks to Travis and Elizabeth Simonds; Sherwood Olin; Fred and Nancy Finnemore; Todd and Rebecca Finnemore-Katz; Ed and Maria Hall; Bob and Linda Wagner; Nina Gilkenson; Fred Field; Bryce, Dianne, and Olivia Leavitt; Chris and Annemarie Sacco; Guy Silvestro; Sarah McCarthy; Alan Lowe; Bo Gallup; Linda Maynard; Jai Bradford; and my sweet nugget, Ashley.

Special thanks to my editor, Karin Womer, and to photographer Joe Corrado and designer Lynda Chilton for the time, energy, and creativity they have put into this project. You rock!

Savor. Linger. Enjoy!

CONTENTS

Introduction
7

The The Cookie Jar
9

Pies, Crisps, and Cobblers
13

Cakes and Cheesecakes
45

Frostings and Fillings
65

Custards, Crullers, and Other Treats
74

Enhancements
89

Classic Candies
99

Appendix: Specialty Products from Maine Producers
105

Recipe Index
107

INTRODUCTION

Memories and Ingredients from Home

Maine is a place steeped in tradition. Family recipes are kept alive for generations, evolving with time. What better way to share the feelings of the past than with the heritage and memories of its flavors. The scent of baking applesauce cake translates easily from one decade to the next. Chocolate chip cookies right out of the oven always put a smile on a child's face. The aromas can transport us back. Although my great grandmother cooked on a woodstove and I with propane, the results, I hope, would make her proud.

The ingredients of Maine and northern New England are found throughout *Delicious Maine Desserts*. They have an integral impact on the final outcome. A cake made with imitation vanilla, margarine, and poor quality flour will taste different from one made with real vanilla extract, fresh Maine butter, and excellent King Arthur flour from Vermont. Glorious Maine blueberries, raspberries, apples, and honey infuse these recipes with a purity only found here. Although these items may cost more than their substitutes, it is better to make a smaller amount that tastes exquisite than a bucketful that is just okay. I think that when we eat fake food, we end up eating more, because it doesn't satisfy.

I appreciate what it costs to feed a family—and I never take that for granted. At the same time, I know that local is better. I would rather buy from the farmers' market or the Rising Tide food co-op here in Damariscotta, than the big box store. It's closer. The food is better, and I am super aware that a choice to use my dollar here keeps the local economy alive. Find your local suppliers. They will help you acquire the best ingredients possible to please your family's palates.

The Happy Ending to a Maine Meal

We have a short growing season here in the Northeast. Fruits and berries come into season during the precious sun-kissed months of summer. Berries of gold, blushing and brilliant crimson, indigo, and deep purple are found under leaf and adorning vine—juicy jewels to be treasured on the tongue.

Maine is known for its blueberries, but did you know that raspberries, blackberries, and strawberries are readily available at farm stands throughout their growing season? Honey is harvested at apiaries throughout the state. All over Maine, maple trees are tapped and their sugary sap boiled down to create that golden delicacy that is real maple syrup.

Remembering to put away some of the bounty is the key to year-round delicacies. Most berries can be frozen or made into sauces, jams, and jellies. (Take a look at the Maine Department of Agriculture's Seasonal Availability Chart at www.getrealmaine.com/connect/farm-share/veggiechart.html.) Enjoy the fruits of the season when they are *in season,* but also buy extra when they're at their freshest for preserving or processing. There is something special about strawberry shortcake in January or blueberry pie in March.

Moderation and the Three-Bite Rule

Dessert is here to stay. No matter how many diet trends and fads appear on the scene, the inevitable sweet ending to a meal will live on. I see some encouraging signs that, as a culture, we are beginning to recognize that moderation is the key. Let's move forward into this book armed with the determination to eat whatever we want—and with the strength of mind to be sensible about it.

Moderation emphasizes quality over quantity. A friend once told me that the perfect dessert size was just three bites: the first to taste the delicious flavors, the second to enjoy the texture, and the third to savor the *mmm, mmm, mmm.*

Dessert should be the last beautiful chord of music before the vibrations of a great meal are relinquished to your heart. As a swing dancer, I love the last strain of a song, when you add a dramatic flourish to complete your dance. It's the icing on the cake, the cherry on top, our just desserts.

Moderation also applies to our pace of life, and that affects our enjoyment of what we eat. Cook together. Take your time when you eat. Shut off the TV. Talk with your family. Chew your food well. Savor a little bit instead of gorging a lot. The slower we eat, the more we taste and appreciate our food. Dessert is a luxury; let's treat it that way.

Notes about Ingredients and Equipment

- **Flour** is all-purpose, (unless stated otherwise) —King Arthur Flour, a New England company, offers an excellent selection of unbleached, unbromated flours.

- **Sugar** is white granulated (unless stated otherwise).

- **Brown Sugar** can be either light or dark (unlesss stated otherwise).

- **Butter** is unsalted.

- **Milk** is whole.

- **Cocoa** is unsweetened powder.

- **Baking pan liners.** Silicone baking sheet liners give all of the advantages of parchment paper with much less waste.

- **Electric mixers.** I grew up with an electric-mixer-using mama, and I learned the benefits of quick creaming and easy whipping at an early age. I love my stand mixer—it reduces the work of most recipes. It is fine to make these recipes with just bowl and spoon, however—it just takes a bit more time and muscle.

Fruit-for-Fat Substitute for Oil and Butter

Use this paste instead of fat in cookies and cakes. The results will be moist and delicious. Use a half cup for every cup of fat in your recipe.

> 16 oz pitted prunes
> 4 c chopped, peeled, cored apples
> 1 c water

Place all ingredients in a medium-size heavy-bottomed saucepan. Cook 15 minutes over medium heat, stirring often. Add more water if the mixture becomes too dry. The fruit will cook down and lose its shape. Purée in a food processor until completely smooth. Store in a covered jar in the refrigerator for up to one month.

THE COOKIE JAR

Cookies just might be my favorite dessert. Crispy and soft, creamy and crunchy— they bridge the spectrum with intense flavors and a variety of textures. I love cookies! Here are some traditional recipes with a twist.

Whoopie Pies

Whoopie pies are a Maine tradition—fluffy frosting sandwiched between two cake-like cookies. (If you plan ahead and bake an odd number of cookie pieces, then you'll get to top the last one with filling and immediately pop it into your mouth. Ah, the sweet rewards.)

Most folks agree that the cakey cookie should be moist, yet sturdy enough to hold on to. The filling, however, is subject to much controversy. There are many secret recipes for creating the luscious, creamy, fluffy white stuff that acts as cookie glue. Some like the kind made with Marshmallow Fluff, some a buttery frosting, and others a tooth-achingly sweet shortening confection.

Recipes have sprung up over the years to satisfy the palates of gourmets and gourmands alike. Here are a few of my favorite insides and outsides. Use your imagination to create the combinations *your* family will love. For a variation, bake the batter in cake pans until a tester comes out clean. Frost the cakes with your favorite whoopie filling. Our kids have always loved "inside out" whoopie pies.

For grownups who love these classic treats, serve whoopie pies with any of the dark-roasted coffee varieties from Coffee By Design (see appendix).

Chocolate Whoopie Pies with Vanilla Cream or Peanut Butter Filling

K nowing how popular whoopie pies are with children, I'm sure peanut butter must have been one of the first alternative flavors for the filling.

Makes a dozen 2-inch whoopie pies

1 c butter
2 c sugar
3 eggs
2 egg yolks
2 t vanilla extract
4 c flour
3 t baking soda
½ t salt
1½ c unsweetened cocoa
1 c buttermilk
1 c sour cream
½ c hot water

Preheat oven to 350 degrees F.

In the bowl of an electric mixer, cream together the butter and sugar. Add the eggs and yolks one at a time and beat until combined. Add the vanilla and beat until combined. Scrape down the sides of the bowl.

Sift together the flour, baking soda, salt, and cocoa. Whisk together the buttermilk and sour cream. Add the sifted dry ingredients to creamed butter mixture alternately with the liquid. Add the hot water slowly and mix until incorporated.

Use an ice cream scoop or a tablespoon to drop the batter 2 inches apart on a greased baking sheet or one lined with a silicone mat or parchment paper.

Bake 10 to 14 minutes or until tops are springy. Cool completely before removing the cookies from the pan or parchment paper.

When assembling the whoopie pies, make the filling layer about ½ inch thick. Wrap whoopies individually in plastic wrap.

Vanilla Cream Filling:
¾ c unsalted butter
2½ c confectioners' sugar, sifted
pinch of salt
4 t vanilla extract
2 t fresh lemon juice
2 egg whites

In the bowl of an electric mixer, cream the butter with the confectioners' sugar and salt until light and fluffy. Add vanilla and lemon juice and mix.

Add the egg whites one at a time, beating thoroughly after each one. The filling will seem to "break," but just keep going; it will come back together. Continue beating until very light and fluffy—as long as 5 minutes.

Peanut Butter Filling:
1 c creamy peanut butter
½ c unsalted butter, softened
1 c confectioners' sugar
1 t vanilla extract
pinch of salt

In the bowl of an electric mixer, beat together until creamy, then continue beating for 4 minutes more on high until the mixture is fluffy and light.

Pumpkin Whoopie Pies with Maple Spice Filling

The pumpkin makes these cakey cookies very moist. These whoopie pies are reminiscent of pumpkin bread with a sweet cinnamon-y frosting. They pair nicely with Sweetgrass Winery's Apple Wine (see appendix).

Makes 8 to 10 2-inch whoopie pies

1 c sugar
1 c maple sugar
1 c melted butter
3 eggs
2 c cooked puréed pumpkin
2 c flour
½ t salt
½ t baking powder
1 t baking soda
2 t cinnamon
1 t ground nutmeg

Preheat oven to 350 degrees F.

Stir together white sugar, maple sugar, butter, and eggs. Add pumpkin. In a separate bowl, sift together the remaining ingredients. Add to the pumpkin mixture and stir just until incorporated. Scrape down the bowl well and stir again to be sure the ingredients are evenly distributed.

Use an ice cream scoop or a large spoon to drop the batter 2 inches apart on a greased baking sheet or one lined with a silicone mat or parchment paper. (My favorite scoop size for whoopie pies is 2 ounces, which is equal to about 3 heaping tablespoons.)

Bake 10 to 14 minutes or until tops are springy and light brown. Remove from the pan by lifting the sheet of silicone or parchment onto a rack.

Cool completely before removing the cookies. To assemble, place a heaping scoop of filling on the flat side of one cookie. The filling layer should be about a half-inch thick. Top with another cookie. Wrap whoopies individually in plastic wrap.

Maple Spice Filling:

¾ c unsalted butter
2½ c confectioners' sugar, sifted
1 t cinnamon
¼ t freshly grated nutmeg
pinch of salt
1 T vanilla extract
2 T Maine maple syrup
2 t fresh lemon juice
2 egg whites

In the bowl of an electric mixer, cream the butter with the confectioners' sugar, cinnamon, nutmeg, and salt until light and fluffy. Add vanilla, maple syrup, and lemon juice, and mix until combined.

Add the egg whites one at a time, beating thoroughly after each one. The filling will seem to "break," but just keep going and whisk away; it will come back together. Scrape down the sides of the bowl. Continue beating until very light and fluffy, as long as 5 minutes.

Banana Whoopie Pies with Cream Cheese Filling

Whenever I have bananas that are too ripe, I peel them, pop them in plastic zip bags, and toss them into the freezer. When it's time to make banana bread or whoopie pies, they come out of the icebox and thaw before they go into the recipe.

Makes a dozen 1½-inch whoopie pies

6 ripe bananas
1½ c sugar
1 egg
2 T buttermilk
½ c vegetable oil
2 t vanilla extract
4½ c flour
1 t baking powder
2 t baking soda

Preheat oven to 350 degrees F.

Peel the bananas and mash them in a large mixing bowl with a potato masher or fork until they are the consistency of pudding. Add sugar, egg, buttermilk, oil, and vanilla. Mix until combined. Sift together the remaining ingredients and add to the batter. Mix well.

Using an ice cream scoop or large spoon, drop the batter onto a greased cookie sheet or one lined with parchment paper or a silicone mat. Bake 15 minutes or until tops are springy and light brown. Remove whole parchment sheet or silicone mat to rack. Cool completely.

To Assemble:

Place a heaping scoop of filling on flat side of one cookie. The filling layer should be about a half-inch thick. Top with another cookie. Wrap whoopies individually in plastic wrap.

Cream Cheese Filling:

1 c unsalted butter
1 c cream cheese
2 t vanilla extract
6 c confectioners' sugar
2 t milk

In the bowl of an electic mixer, beat butter and cream cheese until smooth. Add vanilla. Alternately add sugar and milk. Scrape down the sides of the bowl. Beat 5 minutes until very fluffy.

Bakkles with Vanilla Sugar

Abakkle is a fried cookie. Great-Grammy Letteney made them every year for Christmas. She was very particular about how thin the dough should be rolled before it was cut, and how long they should be cooked. Now our daughter Elizabeth makes the bakkles. She rolls them just right, and I'm sure she will carry on this tradition. *NOTE*: Dough requires 1 hour or more to chill.

Makes 6 dozen or more small cookies

4 cardamom pods or 1 t ground cardamom
6 egg yolks
6 T heavy cream
6 T sugar
1 t lemon extract
1 t brandy or rum
2 c cake flour or all-purpose flour
vegetable oil or shortening for frying

You can make these with an electric mixer, but the directions here are for mixing by hand.

If using whole cardamom pods, remove the seeds, discard the pods, and grind the seeds with a mortar and pestle to a very fine powder.

In a large bowl, beat the egg yolks until light and creamy, about five minutes. Add the heavy cream, one tablespoon at a time, beating well after each addition. Add sugar, one tablespoon at a time, beating well after each addition. Beat in the ground cardamom, lemon extract, and brandy. Add the flour and stir until combined.

Knead the dough on a lightly floured surface until it blisters. Chill at least one hour or overnight.

To shape the bakkles, cut the dough into 6 pieces. On a very lightly floured surface, roll out each piece as thin as possible. Cut the dough into 4 by 2-inch diamonds. Make a 1-inch slit in the lower third of each diamond. Draw the opposite end through the slit. Put 3 inches of vegetable oil or shortening in a heavy-bottomed pan, and heat until it reaches 375 degrees F. Drop the cookies carefully, one by one, into the hot fat. Do not crowd the pan.

The cookies will sink to the bottom and then rise to the surface. Once on the surface, let cook for 15 seconds or so, until slightly brown. Turn. Let cook another 10 to 15 seconds. Remove and drain on a tray lined with brown paper or paper towels. Sprinkle with vanilla sugar or confectioners' sugar. Cool.

Store in a tin or airtight container lined with waxed paper.

Vanilla Sugar:

> 1 vanilla bean
> 2 c granulated sugar

Set the vanilla bean on a cutting board and slice it down the center. Using the back of a knife, scrape the seeds out of the bean. Stir the vanilla bean seeds thoroughly into the sugar. Bury the rest of the bean in the center of the sugar and seal tightly in an airtight container.

You can use the sugar right away or let it sit for one to two weeks in a cool dry place for stronger flavor. Use as you would regular granulated sugar.

Jumbo Sour Cream Softies

Scrumptious and moist, these soft-baked cookies are wonderful with coffee, tea, or milk.
Makes 30 cookies

½ c unsalted butter
1½ c sugar
2 eggs
1 t vanilla extract
3 c flour
½ t salt
½ t baking soda
½ t baking powder
1 c sour cream

Topping:
¼ c sugar
1 T cinnamon

Preheat oven to 400 degrees F.

In the bowl of an electric mixer, cream together butter and sugar. Add eggs and vanilla. Stir until combined. In a separate bowl, sift together the flour, salt, baking soda, and baking powder. Add to the butter mixture. Scrape down the sides of the bowl and beat again until completely combined. Drop by tablespoon onto ungreased cookie sheet 4 inches apart.

Stir together the sugar and cinnamon topping and sprinkle mixture on top of cookies. Bake 10 to 12 minutes or until just barely golden. Cool on a wire rack. Store in an airtight container.

Ultra Nutty Hermits

This is a new variation on a very old recipe. The dough for hermits is formed into long strips on a cookie sheet, baked, and then sliced into cookies. They stay very moist and chewy.

Makes approximately 2 dozen

1 c sugar
1 c brown sugar, packed
1 c butter
2 eggs
1 t vanilla extract
½ c chopped walnuts
½ c chopped pecans
½ c chopped almonds
½ c shredded coconut
1 c raisins, plus water to cover
1 t baking soda
1 t cinnamon
3 c flour
½ t salt

Preheat oven to 375 degrees F.

Line a baking sheet with parchment pager or silicone mat.

Cream white sugar, brown sugar, and butter. Add eggs and vanilla. Place raisins in a small saucepan, cover with water, and simmer for 5 minutes. Drain, reserving ⅓ cup of the raisin water. Stir baking soda into water.

Add raisins to creamed butter mixture. Sift together the cinnamon, salt and flour. Add dry ingredients alternately with soda water. Stir in nuts and coconut. Shape dough into 1½ x 2-inch strips that run the length of the baking pan. Place on lined pan and bake for 10 minutes. Cool 10 minutes. While still warm, cut each strip into cookies the size you desire.

Glazed Oatmeal Apricot Drops

These cookies can be made with chopped dried cherries, currants, cranberries, golden raisins, apricots (my favorite), or substitute chocolate chunks.

Makes 30 cookies

¾ c unsalted butter at room temperature
3 T chunky apricot jam
¾ c brown sugar
½ c sugar
1 egg
1 c flour
½ t baking soda
1 t salt
3 c instant or regular rolled oats
¼ c buttermilk
1 t vanilla extract
1 c finely chopped dried apricots or other fruit

Preheat oven to 350 degrees F.

In a medium bowl, cream together the butter, apricot jam, brown sugar, and white sugar. Add egg and beat well. In a separate bowl, sift together the flour, baking soda, and salt. Stir in the oats. In a measuring cup, stir together the buttermilk and vanilla. Add the dry ingredients and buttermilk alternately to the butter mixture, stirring well after each addition. Scrape down the sides of the bowl and stir again to be sure the ingredients are completely incorporated. Add the dried apricots and stir until evenly distributed throughout the batter.

Drop using an ice cream scoop or by the tablespoon onto an ungreased or parchment-lined cookie sheet, about 2 inches apart. Bake 12 to 15 minutes or until golden.

Icing:
  2 T buttermilk
  1½ c confectioners' sugar

Whisk together buttermilk and confectioners' sugar until smooth. If necessary, add another teaspoon of buttermilk to create a smooth consistency. Drizzle icing over warm cookies, then cool cookies completely. Icing will harden slightly. Store in airtight container.

Biscotti

The name *biscotti* means "twice baked" in Italian. If you are eating just one, you have a biscotto. More than one, you've got biscotti. These crunchy cookies are perfect with a cup of espresso. Coffee By Design, in Portland, has a wonderful espresso roast that complements these recipes lusciously. As an after-dinner sweet, serve biscotti with a dessert wine from Winterport Winery. Sweetgrass Farm Winery's Three Crow Rum also pairs well with biscotti. (See appendix for information about these Maine businesses.)

Shaping and Baking Foolproof Biscotti

Divide the prepared biscotti dough in half. Line a cookie sheet with parchment paper or a silicone baking mat. On the lined pan, form the dough into two rectangles 12 inches long by 2 to 3 inches wide, leaving 2 inches between them. Bake for 25 minutes or until golden brown.

Remove the rectangles from the pan and cool on a wire rack for 10 minutes. Using a long serrated knife, cut the rectangles on a slight diagonal into ¾-inch slices (you should get about 12 from each rectangle). Using the same cookie sheet, set a cooling rack on top of the parchment or silicone baking mat. Carefully place the cut cookies on the rack, next to each other but not touching. Bake again for 12 to 15 minutes or until firm.

If you do not have wire racks, bake the cookies on lined pans for 6 minutes. Turn the cookies over and bake for another 6 to 9 minutes or until firm. Remove from the oven and let cool.

Store in an airtight container. They will keep for a month, but are best eaten within the first week.

Fruit and Nut Biscotti

This recipe doubles well and adapts to the flavors you love. I often combine white chocolate, almonds, and coconut or pistachio; cranberry and orange; or lemon and lavender.
Makes 2 dozen

1 c unsalted butter at room temperature

1 c white or light brown sugar

4 eggs

1 T extract or liqueur: vanilla, anise, almond, Calvados, Cognac, or your favorite

1 T grated fresh lemon or orange zest, finely chopped citron, or grated fresh ginger (optional)

2 T seeds: poppy, flax, sesame, caraway, or fennel

1½ t ground cinnamon, ginger, cardamom, thyme, lavender, or your favorite

½ t salt

1½ t baking powder

3¾ c all-purpose flour

½ c finely chopped dried fruit or chopped chocolate

½ c finely chopped nuts: pine nuts, pecans, walnuts, coconut, pistachios, macadamias, or a combination

Preheat oven to 350 degrees F.

In the bowl of a mixer, cream together the butter and sugar until light and fluffy. Scrape down the sides of the bowl. Add the eggs one at a time, beating well after each addition. Add the extract, zest, and seeds. Beat until well combined.

In a separate bowl, sift together the spice, salt, baking powder, and flour. Add to the butter mixture and beat, scraping down the bowl with a spatula, just until completely combined. Mix in the dried fruit and nuts.

Shape and bake the biscotti as described on page 18.

Triple Chocolate Biscotti

1¾ c flour
⅓ c unsweetened cocoa
2 t baking powder
½ t salt
6 T unsalted butter
1 c sugar
3 eggs
2 t vanilla extract
1 c dark chocolate bits
½ c white chocolate bits

Preheat oven to 350 degrees F.

Sift together the flour, cocoa, baking powder, and salt. In a medium bowl, cream the butter and sugar until light and fluffy. Add eggs one at a time, beating well after each addition. Stir in vanilla. Add the flour mixture and beat, scraping down the bowl with a spatula, just until completely combined. Mix in the dark and white chocolate bits.

Shape and bake the biscotti as described on page 18.

Intense Ginger Biscotti

¾ c unsalted butter at room temperature
¾ c light brown sugar
3 eggs
1 T vanilla extract
1 T grated fresh ginger root
2 T golden flax seed
1 t ground ginger
¼ t salt
¼ t ground black pepper
1 t baking powder
3¼ c all-purpose flour
½ c finely chopped crystallized ginger

Preheat oven to 350 degrees F.

In the bowl of a mixer, cream together the butter and brown sugar until light and fluffy. Scrape down the sides of the bowl. Add the eggs one at a time, beating well after each addition. Add the vanilla, fresh ginger, and flax seed. Beat until well combined.

In a separate bowl, sift together the ground ginger, salt, pepper, baking powder, and flour. Add the flour mixture to the butter mixture and beat, scraping down the bowl with a spatula, just until completely combined. Mix in the crystallized ginger.

Shape and bake the biscotti as described on page 18.

Cookie Pizzas

This recipe is fantastic for birthdays and other celebrations. Feel free to decorate with the treats of your choice. I like to slice up candy bars and lay the pieces on top, like pepperoni on a regular pizza. It's also great made into 3-inch cookies as individual pizzas for parties. Multiply the recipe to make enough dough and allow your guests to decorate their own.

Makes 12 "pizza slices" or cookies

½ c butter
¾ c brown sugar
1 egg
1 t vanilla extract
¾ c flour
pinch of salt
½ t baking powder
½ t baking soda
1 c instant or regular rolled oats
¼ c water
½ c shredded coconut (sweetened
  or unsweetened)

Decorations:

1/2 c nuts
1/2 c shredded coconut (sweetened
  or unsweetened)
1 c chocolate bits
½ c M&Ms

Preheat oven to 350 degrees F.

In a medium bowl cream together the butter and sugar. Add egg and vanilla. Beat well. In a separate bowl sift together the flour, salt, baking powder, and baking soda. Stir in the oats. Add the dry ingredients and water alternately to the butter mixture, stirring well after each addition. Scrape down the sides of the bowl and stir again to be sure the ingredients are completely incorporated.

Turn out the dough onto a parchment-lined cookie sheet. Press the dough into a ½-inch thick, 12-inch diameter "pizza crust." Sprinkle with nuts and coconut, leaving a plain edge ¾ inch wide to resemble the edge of a pizza. Decorate with chocolate bits and M&Ms. Bake 20 minutes or until edges are golden but not brown. The coconut will brown very slightly. (Bake 12 to 14 minutes for individual pizzas.)

Remove from oven. Using a large pizza cutter or knife, slice the cookie pizza-style into 12 pieces while still warm.

Pecan or Flax Meltaway Cookies

These nutty little cookies melt in your mouth. Enjoy them with a cup of tea. Use either chopped nuts or flax seeds to add body and crunch to the delicate dough. Sweetgrass Farm Winery and Distillery (see appendix) sells a wonderful pure vanilla extract with a lovely strong flavor that adds depth to any cookie recipe.

Makes approximately 2 dozen

1 cup butter
1 cup confectioners' sugar
1 teaspoon vanilla extract
1 T Cognac or brandy
1 egg yolk
2 c flour
½ c finely chopped pecans or whole flax seeds
additional confectioners' sugar for sprinkling

In the bowl of an electric mixer, cream together the butter and sugar. Add vanilla, Cognac, and egg yolk. Scrape down the sides of the bowl and beat two minutes. Gradually stir in the flour until completely combined. Add nuts or flax seeds and stir until evenly blended. Form dough into a ball, wrap, and chill for 2 to 3 hours.

Preheat oven to 325 degrees F.

Pinch off 2-inch pieces of dough and roll them into balls. Place on an ungreased cookie sheet and flatten slightly with the palm of your hand or the bottom of a glass. Bake 15 minutes or until firmly set but not brown.

Roll in confectioners' sugar while hot. Cool. Roll in confectioners' sugar again and store in an airtight container until ready to serve.

Mom's Traditional Chocolate Chip Cookies

My mom made these delectable, soft-on-the-inside, crunchy-on-the-outside cookies on a regular basis, but never without me absconding with a good portion of the dough. This dough may be baked as drop cookies or squares and also freezes extremely well.

Makes 2 dozen (depending on how much dough actually gets baked…)

1 c brown sugar
½ c sugar
½ c butter
½ c shortening
1½ t vanilla extract
2 eggs
2½ c flour
1 t baking soda
½ t salt
1 (12 oz) package chocolate chips
1 c nuts (optional)

If you plan to bake your cookies right away, preheat oven to 350 degrees F.

Cream together the brown sugar, white sugar, butter, and shortening until light and fluffy. Add vanilla. Add eggs one at a time, beating thoroughly after each. In a separate bowl, sift together flour, baking soda, and salt. Stir the flour mixture into the sugar-and-butter mixture until well blended. Stir in chocolate bits. Add nuts if you like—pecans and macadamia nuts are especially good. Scrape down the sides of your bowl to be sure all the goodies are incorporated into the dough.

At this point you have two options: round cookies or squares.

For round drop cookies, line a baking sheet with parchment or a silicone baking mat. By using an ice cream scoop—the kind with a moving release band inside the scoop—you can drop the batter onto the baking sheet easily in consistent amounts. Baking time will vary depending on the size of your scoop. For a 2-ounce scoop, drop the cookies about 2 inches apart, and bake for 8 to 10 minutes, or until golden brown.

For squares, spread the dough into a greased 9 by 13-inch baking pan. Bake for 25 minutes or until the center is lightly browned. Cool a bit, then cut into 2-inch squares. (These make wonderful ice cream sandwiches. Place a cooled square on a plate, top with a scoop of your favorite ice cream, and cover with another square. For the deluxe version, drizzle with Hot Fudge Sauce [page 90]. Yum!)

This dough freezes extremely well. If you want to save some to bake later, spoon or scoop cookie-sized balls of dough onto a pan lined with plastic wrap. Top with another piece of plastic wrap and place in your freezer. After the dough balls have hardened, transfer them into a plastic zip-close freezer bag. The frozen dough will store indefinitely. (This is a dangerous thing to do if you like to snack on unbaked cookie dough; removing one from the freezer to eat frozen is a treat anytime.) You can bake the drop cookies straight from the freezer. Just keep an eye on them, as they take a little longer to bake.

Maple Sugar Crusted Gingersnaps

Gingersnaps are molasses spice cookies that, when paired with maple sugar, give off a tantalizing scent while baking. They make me think of gingerbread men and morning pancakes all wrapped up into one glorious cookie. *NOTE:* Dough requires a 2-hour chill time before baking.

Makes 3 dozen

¾ c unsalted butter
1 c sugar
1 egg
¼ c molasses
2 c flour
2 t baking soda
½ t salt
1 t ground ginger
1 t cinnamon
½ t ground black pepper
½ c maple sugar

In the bowl of an electric mixer, cream together the butter and sugar until light and fluffy. Scrape down the sides of the bowl. Add the egg. Beat well. Add the molasses. Beat until well combined. In a separate bowl, sift together the flour, baking soda, salt, ground ginger, cinnamon, and pepper. Add the flour mixture to the mixer bowl and mix, scraping down the bowl with a spatula, just until completely combined. Cover and chill 2 hours or overnight.

Preheat oven to 350 degrees F.

Place maple sugar in a bowl. Break off pieces of dough that are about the size of a whole walnut. Shape into a ball. Roll ball in maple sugar. Place sugared dough balls on an ungreased cookie sheet, 2 inches apart. Flatten dough balls to ½-inch thick. Bake for 10 minutes. Cool on wire rack.

Cutout Vanilla Bean Cookies

This recipe requires 2 hours to chill the dough before baking. Try with Sweetgrass Winery's varnilla extract for outstanding flavor (see appendix).

Makes 4 dozen

1 vanilla bean
1 lb unsalted butter
1½ c sugar
½ t salt
3 t vanilla extract
2 egg yolks
4 c all-purpose flour
½ c jam: lingonberry, sour cherry, hot pepper, beach plum, or your choice

Slice vanilla bean in half lengthwise. With the dull side of a knife, scrape the seeds out of the bean and set aside. Reserve the bean pod for making Vanilla Sugar (page 15). In a large bowl, cream together the butter, sugar, salt, and vanilla seeds and extract until smooth and light. Mix in the egg yolks until well combined, scraping down the sides of the bowl often. Add the flour and mix just until incorporated. Turn out onto a lightly floured board and knead a few times, until you have a smooth dough.

Place on a sheet of plastic wrap and roll into a log. Wrap and chill for 2 hours or freeze.

When you are ready to bake, preheat the oven to 325 degrees F. Line your cookie sheets with parchment or a silicone baking mat.

Roll out the dough on a lightly floured board to ¼-inch thick and cut into 3-inch circles or squares. Drop a teaspoon of jam into the center of each cookie. Fold each cookie in half and press edges to seal. Place cookies 1 inch apart on a cookie sheet. Bake 16 to 18 minutes or until the edges just begin to turn light brown. Do not overbake.

Double Peanut Butter Chocolate-Flecked Shortbread

These delicious old favorites have a chocolaty-peanut butter surprise in the middle. By adding finely chopped chocolate to the dough, you get the best combination of flavors. Using butter makes a softer cookie. Vegetable shortening makes it crisper and more crumbly. You can make this recipe dairy free by using vegetable shortening and substituting water for the milk. *NOTE:* Requires 2-hour chill time before baking.

Makes 2 dozen cookies

1 c sugar
1 c butter or vegetable shortening
1 c plus ¼ c creamy peanut butter
½ c light corn syrup
1 t baking soda
1 t salt
3 c flour
2 T milk or cream
½ c finely chopped bittersweet chocolate
¼ c chopped chocolate bits

In a medium bowl, cream together the sugar, butter or shortening, and 1 cup of peanut butter. Add the corn syrup and beat two minutes. Scrape down the sides of the bowl. Add the baking soda, salt, and flour. Mix until completely combined. Stir in the milk and bittersweet chocolate. Divide the dough in half and shape into two rolls 2 inches in diameter. Wrap and chill until firm.

When you're ready to bake, preheat oven to 350 degrees F.

In a small bowl, combine the chopped chocolate bits and ¼ cup peanut butter. Slice the dough into ¼-inch-thick coins. Place half of the coins on two greased or parchment- or silicone-lined cookie sheets. They can be set ½ inch apart as they do not expand much. Top each slice with a scant teaspoon of the chocolate-peanut butter mixture. Place another cookie coin on top of each. Using a fork, press down around the edges of each cookie to seal in the filling. Bake 12 minutes or until light brown.

Knock-Your-Socks-Off Brownies

These are my dad's favorites. Dark, moist, and chewy, they are a chocolaty treat. This recipe is great baked in a 9 by 13-inch pan or in tiny muffin tins for little bites. Topped with chocolate, they are fit for a king—just like Dad. Either way, they're great for bake sales and fundraisers.

Makes 24 squares

1 c butter
6 oz unsweetened baking chocolate
4 eggs
2 c sugar
1 c flour
¼ c unsweetened cocoa
½ t salt
6 oz semisweet chocolate bits

Preheat oven to 350 degrees F.

Melt butter and unsweetened chocolate in a double boiler. Set aside until cool. Beat eggs with sugar until thickened. Add cooled butter mixture. Stir until completely smooth. Add flour, cocoa, and salt. Stir until incorporated. Fold in chocolate bits.

Line a greased 9 by 13-inch pan with parchment paper or foil and grease well. Spread batter evenly into pan. Bake for 25 minutes.

Cool for 10 minutes. Run a sharp knife around the edges of the pan to release the sheet of brownies. Lift it out in one piece and cool completely (unless you can't resist, then have a little piece—it melts in your mouth when it's warm). Gently peel off paper or foil and slice into 24 pieces (4 across, 6 down).

To bake them as tiny muffins, spray or grease the muffin pans thoroughly or line with muffin cups. Bake 12 to 15 minutes and check for doneness by inserting a toothpick or tester—it should come out with moist crumbs. Sprinkle each with a few chocolate bits for an added touch.

When they are completely cool you can wrap them up and freeze for up to a week.

They are great alone or as part of a sundae. Instead of cutting the baked brownie into squares, use a small cookie cutter and dip the pieces in melted chocolate.

One other option: When the brownies come out of the oven, sprinkle chocolate bits, peanut butter bits, or unwrapped Andes-style chocolate mints on top. The heat will melt the toppings. Spread the melted bits or mints over the top and let cool.

Pumpkin Bars with Streusel Topping

Pumpkin pie meets blond brownies. Drizzle them with caramel sauce or give them a dollop of whipped cream—either way they are delicious. These bars pair well with Sweetgrass Winery's Three Crow Rum (see appendix).

Makes 24 squares

Crust and topping:
- 1 c regular rolled oats
- 1 c brown sugar
- ¼ t fine sea salt
- 1 t cinnamon
- 1½ c flour
- 1 c butter
- ½ c chopped pecans (optional)

Filling:
- 2 c cooked, puréed pumpkin
- 3 eggs
- 2 T molasses
- 1¼ c evaporated milk
- ¾ c sugar
- 1 T flour
- ½ t salt
- 1 t vanilla extract
- 2 t cinnamon
- 1 t confectioners' ginger
- ½ t cardamom

Preheat oven to 375 degrees F and grease a 9 by 13-inch inch pan with butter.

In a medium bowl, stir together the oats, brown sugar, salt, cinnamon and flour. Cut in the butter until it resembles coarse crumbs. Gather into a ball and divide mixture, reserving one third.

Press two thirds of mixture evenly in the bottom of the baking pan, coming 1 inch up the sides. Bake 15 minutes.

To make the filling, combine the pumpkin, eggs, molasses, evaporated milk, sugar, flour, salt, vanilla, cinnamon, ginger, and cardamom in a medium bowl. Whisk until smooth. Pour over partially baked crust. Smooth the filling. Bake 20 minutes and remove from the oven.

Crumble the remaining crust mixture, distributing it evenly on top of the filling. Return to the oven and bake another 20 minutes or until a knife inserted in the center comes out clean. Cool 10 minutes. Slice into squares. Serve with Maple Caramel Sauce (page 43) or Maple Chantilly Cream (page 86).

Blond Butterscotch Brownies

These soft brown sugar bars are studded with chocolate. Just barely baked, they are dense and delicious, almost penuche-like. For Maine-made apple butter, I like the Pastor Chuck Orchards brand (see appendix).
Makes 24 squares

¼ c butter, melted
¼ c apple butter
2 c light brown sugar
2 t vanilla extract
2 eggs
1½ c flour
¼ t salt
2 t baking powder
½ c chocolate bits
½ c butterscotch bits

Preheat oven to 350 degrees F.

In a large bowl, stir together butter, apple butter, sugar, and vanilla. Add eggs one at a time, beating well after each addition. Stir in flour, salt, and baking powder. Pour batter evenly into greased 9 by 13-inch pan. Sprinkle top with chocolate and butterscotch bits.

Bake 30 minutes or just until done. Do not overbake. Cool and cut into 24 squares.

Choco-spresso Bars

Coffee By Design, in Portland, (see appendix) roasts the most delicious espresso bean blend. Brew up a few cups of espresso and enjoy one yourself while you make this delicious mocha-glazed dessert.

Makes 32 bars

½ c butter
4 oz unsweetened baking chocolate
3 T brewed espresso or strong coffee
3 eggs
1 c sugar
½ c flour
4 T unsweetened cocoa
¼ t salt
¼ c semisweet chocolate bits

Preheat oven to 350 degrees F.

Grease an 8 by 8-inch pan. Melt butter and unsweetened chocolate in a double boiler. Set aside until cool. Beat eggs with sugar until thickened. Add espresso and cooled butter mixture. Stir until completely smooth. Add flour, cocoa, and salt. Stir until incorporated. Fold in chocolate bits.

Bake 15 to 20 minutes or until a cake tester or toothpick inserted in the center comes out with moist crumbs. Glaze while warm. Let glazed cake cool. Cut into 2- by 1-inch bars.

Espresso Glaze:

2 T freshly brewed espresso or 1½ T hot water
   and 2 t instant espresso powder
1 t vanilla extract
1½ c confectioners' sugar
2 T soft butter
¼ c melted bittersweet chocolate
2 T unsweetened cocoa

Stir all ingredients together until smooth. Drizzle on bars (or your favorite cake) while warm. The glaze will stay slightly oozy, so make sure you have lots of napkins on hand.

The recipe multiplies well, so feel free to make extra glaze for another batch of chocolate squares. Store in refrigerator for up to 3 days.

PIES, CRISPS, AND COBBLERS

A h, the luxurious scent of pies coming out of the oven. Bake a pie for a friend and make a second for yourself—you get to smell the wonderful aroma all the while they're baking.

Maine kitchens are well known for their traditional pies, crisps, and cobblers. The early recipes used no exact measurements. There were references to "butter the size of a hen's egg," We've taken the guesswork out, making it easy to create a taste of Maine in your own modern kitchen.

Foolproof Pie Crust

This recipe makes a wonderful flaky crust. It's worth the effort to make up all this dough, because it keeps for at least two months in the freezer. All you have to do is let the frozen pastry thaw in the refrigerator for a few hours and you're ready to roll.

Makes six single or three double crusts

1 T white vinegar or lemon juice
6 c pastry or all-purpose flour
½ t fine sea salt
1 c vegetable shortening
1 c unsalted butter or lard, very cold, cut into
  ½-inch cubes

Half fill a 2-cup measure with ice cubes. Add 1 tablespoon of vinegar or lemon juice and fill the cup with cold water. Stir and set aside.

In a large bowl, stir together the flour and salt. Add the shortening and cut it into the flour with a pastry blender or two knives until the mixture resembles fine meal. Add the butter or lard and cut it in until the mixture resembles coarse crumbs about the size of peas. Sprinkle ice water, one tablespoon at a time, over about 1 cup of the flour mixture, toss lightly with a fork, and push aside. Repeat

Baking an Unfilled Pastry Crust

To bake an unfilled ("blind") single-crust pie shell, preheat oven to 400 degrees F. Carefully lay the rolled dough in a pie plate and crimp the edges. Cover the bottom with a sheet of parchment. Fill the parchment with dry beans: their weight will prevent the crust from shrinking and puffing in the middle as it bakes. Bake until light golden brown, about 12 minutes. Remove the beans when the crust is done and save them for future pie baking.

until all of the flour mixture is moistened. Add only enough water so that the dough holds together. Stir all the flour together with 10 strokes.

Divide dough into six equal pieces. Form each piece into a ball and flatten into a disk. Wrap each disk tightly in plastic. Chill 1 hour or up to 2 days. (To freeze, place the chilled disks in freezer zip bags.)

When ready to use, allow the chilled dough to sit on the counter for 15 minutes to soften. Roll out on a lightly floured board, a silicone baking mat, or parchment paper. Work quickly and use only enough flour to prevent sticking. Fit into pie plate or tart shell and proceed with your desired recipe.

Butter Crust (Pâte Brisée)

Buttery and crisp, this is the perfect crust for any pie. Work the dough as little as possible to yield a flaky crust. *NOTE:* Dough should be chilled before rolling out.
Makes 2 single crusts

1 c (2 sticks) butter, cut into little pieces
3 T sugar (optional)
3 c pastry or all-purpose flour
2 t salt
1½ t white vinegar
¼ c to ½ c ice water

Cut together the butter, sugar, flour, and salt until the mixture resembles coarse crumbs. Cut in the vinegar. Add ice water 1 tablespoon at a time, stirring just until dough comes together. Divide dough into two pieces. Form each piece into a flattened disk. Cover with plastic wrap and chill until firm.

Remove the dough from the refrigerator and let sit for 10 minutes. Roll out the dough on a lightly floured surface to ⅛ or ¼ inch thick. (To make the process easier, roll out the dough between two pieces of parchment paper. Peel off the top piece of parchment paper and invert the crust onto your pie plate, then peel off the second piece of paper. No fuss—no muss—it is crust!)

Crumb Crusts Galore

Crumb crusts are quick and easy. Different types of crackers, cookies, and pretzels make wonderful crusts. Try graham crackers, cookies such as chocolate or vanilla wafers or gingersnaps, or use your imagination with other crumbs and spices—a sprinkle of cocoa or cinnamon makes a nice variation.

Makes crust for one 9-inch pie or springform pan

1½ c (5 oz) finely ground crumbs
5 T unsalted butter, melted
3 T sugar (or less, to taste)
⅛ t salt

The quantities listed here use a ratio of butter to crumbs that works well with graham crackers and most cookies. Add more butter if you need it to achieve a moist, compressible consistency with other types of crumbs.

Stir ingredients together and press onto the bottom and 1 inch up the side of a 9-inch pie plate or in the bottom of a buttered 10-inch springform pan. Fill right away or chill up to 2 hours.

Black and Blue Berry Slump

A slump is a cooked fruit dish topped with a biscuit-like layer. They're delicious with any type of fruit. Six cups of mix-and-match berries or fruit of your choice, and away you go.

Serves 12

3 c fresh blackberries
3 c fresh Maine blueberries
1 T fresh lime juice
1 c sugar
¼ c brown sugar
1 c all-purpose flour
1½ t baking powder
¼ t salt
¾ c whole milk
3 T unsalted butter, melted
ice cream or whipped cream to accompany

Preheat oven to 375 degrees F.

Place berries in an ungreased 4-quart baking dish and sprinkle with lime juice and sugar. Set aside. Sift together brown sugar, flour, baking powder, and salt. Add milk and butter and whisk until smooth, then pour over berries. The berries may peek through, which is okay.

Place baking dish on a sheet pan. Bake the slump on the middle rack of oven until top is golden, 40 to 45 minutes. Remove from oven and cool 20 minutes. Serve warm with ice cream or whipped cream.

Fruit Tart with Custard Center

This tart is a beautiful way to showcase fresh fruit. Blueberries or strawberries look gorgeous. This cake pairs well with Winterport Winery's Pear Wine (see appendix).

Serves 12

Tart Shell:

1 c all-purpose flour
⅔ c pastry flour
¼ c sugar
8 T butter
3 egg yolks
1 t vanilla extract
½ t water
3 T cream

Custard:

3 c heavy cream
8 egg yolks
1 c sugar
1 T vanilla extract
⅛ t salt
2 T butter for greasing pan

Topping:

2 cups fresh berries or sliced kiwi
¼ c apple jelly (optional)

Preheat oven to 350 degrees F.

In a medium bowl, cut together all-purpose flour, pastry flour, sugar, and butter until the mixture resembles coarse crumbs. Stir in egg yolks, vanilla, and water. If the mixture is too dry, add the cream, a tablespoon at a time. Gather into a ball and flatten into a disk. Wrap and chill 1 hour.

Thoroughly grease a 12-inch tart pan with a removable bottom. Roll out dough on a lightly floured board. Place it in the pan and press gently to form it to the sides. Bake for 10 minutes.

Once the crust is prebaked, whisk all the custard ingredients together. Pour into the partially baked crust. Bake until set, about 30 minutes. Cool. Remove the tart from the pan.

When tart is chilled, cover with plastic wrap and chill for 1 hour. Decorate the top with concentric circles of fresh fruit.

To glaze the top, melt ¼ cup of apple jelly and use it to paint the fruit with a soft bristle or silicone pastry brush.

Rustic Apple and Pear Tart with Cheddar Cheese

Rustic tarts are wonderful and "organic," their shape being determined by how you fold the crust. Sometimes the fruit juice bubbles out while the tart cooks, so use a baking sheet with at least 1-inch sides. The cheddar cheese and fruit mixture is a sweet/salty match made in heaven. This tart pairs well with Cellardoor Vineyard's Riesling wine (see appendix).

Serves 12

8 oz pie dough (enough for a single 9-inch crust), slightly cooler than room temperature
3 c coarsely chopped, cored unpeeled apples
2 c coarsely chopped, cored unpeeled pears
1 T cider
1 T fresh lemon juice
½ c tart or sweet dried cherries
1 c sugar, or to taste
2 T cornstarch
½ t nutmeg
2 t cinnamon
½ t sea salt
½ t ground black pepper
1 egg white
1 t milk
4 oz extra sharp cheddar cheese for garnish

Prepare a pie dough and keep it slightly cooler than room temperature. Preheat oven to 425 degrees F.

Place chopped apple and pear in a large bowl. Pour cider and lemon juice over fruit and toss to coat. Add dried cherries. Mix together sugar, cornstarch, nutmeg, cinnamon, sea salt, and pepper. Reserve ¼ c of the sugar and spice mixture for the topping. Add remaining sugar and spices to fruit and toss well to coat.

Roll out the dough on a very lightly floured board. You'll want a roundish piece 14 to 18 inches in diameter. Place the dough on a baking sheet. Mound the fruit into the center. Gather the crust up and over the fruit. Pinch the edges together, leaving at least 2 inches in the center open so the steam can vent.

In a small bowl, whisk together the egg white and milk. Brush top of pastry with a little of the egg white mixture and sprinkle evenly with the reserved cinnamon sugar. Bake for 30 to 35 minutes or until crust is brown and fruit filling is thick and bubbly.

When ready to serve, finely grate cheddar cheese and mound ¼ cup or so on top of each slice of tart. Serve warm or at room temperature.

Almost Bitter Chocolate Torte with Cappuccino Cream

This multilayered torte makes a spectacular presentation. The salty pretzel crust is a beautiful complement to the dark chocolate center. All in all, it is a decadent match.
Makes one 10-inch torte, serves 20

Crust:
1½ c (5 oz) finely ground pretzel crumbs
5 T unsalted butter, melted
3 T sugar

Filling and Topping:
8 oz finely chopped bittersweet chocolate
4 oz finely chopped unsweetened
   baking chocolate
4 eggs
½ c sugar
½ c cold butter cut into ½-inch cubes
3 t vanilla extract
1 T Kahlua liqueur
1 T Cognac
1 c heavy cream
1 T brewed, cooled espresso

Stir together pretzel crumbs, melted butter, and sugar, and press the mixture into the bottom of a 10-inch springform pan. Chill until ready to fill.

In a double boiler, melt bittersweet and unsweetened chocolates. Add eggs and sugar, whisking constantly until hot. Beat in butter a piece at a time, whisking after each addition. Add vanilla, Kahlua, and Cognac. Whisk for 5 minutes. Pour two thirds of the mixture into the crust and chill.

Allow the remaining third of the chocolate mixture to cool to room temperature.

Whip cream until soft peaks form. Whisk in espresso and cooled chocolate mixture. Continue to beat until completely combined and light. Mound on top of the torte. Chill until ready to serve.

Release sides of the springform pan. Run a knife under the bottom crust and slide onto a cake plate. Allow torte to come up to room temperature before serving. Slice with a sharp knife.

Peanut Butter Mousse Pie

If you are a peanut butter fan, this is the pie for you. The filling is a light peanut butter mousse that tastes great chilled or almost frozen. You can make it a day ahead and the flavors will just get better.
Makes one 9-inch pie, serves 12

Crust:
    6 T butter, plus a bit more for greasing the pan
    1 c chocolate cookie crumbs
    2 T sugar

Filling:
    1 c (8 oz) cream cheese at room temperature
    1 c creamy peanut butter
    2 T softened unsalted butter
    1 c plus 2 T confectioners' sugar
    ½ c heavy cream
    1 T vanilla extract

Topping:
    ½ c heavy cream
    ¾ c semisweet chocolate, finely chopped

Grease a 9-inch pie plate. Melt 6 tablespoons of butter and mix with the cookie crumbs and sugar. Press evenly into the pie plate. Chill one hour.

In the bowl of an electric mixer, cream together the cream cheese, peanut butter, and softened butter. Scrape down the sides of the bowl with a rubber spatula. Gradually add 1 cup confectioners' sugar. Beat until fluffy.

In a separate bowl, whip the cream to soft peaks. Add 2 tablespoons confectioners' sugar and vanilla. Whip to stiff peaks. Fold one third of the whipped cream into the peanut butter mixture. Gently fold in the remaining cream. Spoon into chilled crust. Chill until firm, about three hours.

In a small saucepan, heat the cream to a simmer. Add the chocolate. Stir until smooth and melted. Cool topping to room temperature and spread over pie. Chill again until firm.

Blueberry Peach Crisp

This combination creates a deep purple body and golden brown top. With a dollop of cream it's out of this world.

Serves 8 to 10

4 c sliced fresh peaches
6 c Maine blueberries
3 T fresh lemon juice
1 t vanilla extract
1 c dried cranberries or blueberries
1 c sugar, divided
¼ c cornstarch
1½ c flour
½ c firmly packed brown sugar
1 t cinnamon
1 t nutmeg
½ t salt
1 c unsalted butter, cold
3 T unsalted butter, melted

Preheat oven to 350 degrees F.

Combine peaches, blueberries, lemon juice, dried fruit, and vanilla in a 4-quart or larger baking dish. Toss with ½ cup sugar and cornstarch. Set aside.

In a medium bowl, combine flour, ½ cup sugar, brown sugar, cinnamon, nutmeg, and salt. Cut cold butter into dry ingredients until mixture is crumbly. Sprinkle this topping mixture over fruit and drizzle with the melted butter.

Cover with foil and place on a sheet pan larger than the baking dish. (This recipe is known for bubbling over.) Bake 30 minutes. Uncover and bake 25 to 30 minutes or until top is golden.

Lemon Luscious Torte

My friend Tony Sacco is a baker extraordinaire. I think he just might love to cook as much as I do. Every Thanksgiving, he and his wife Marilyn have a pie party. You might think this would include a few traditional pies and turkey day leftovers… not exactly. Tony makes up dozens of pies of all types and folks flock from miles around to share in this holiday tradition. Here is a variation of his lemon pie with a gracious bow to his culinary prowess. *NOTE:* It is best to prepare the lemon curd and white chocolate mousse a day ahead and chill overnight before assembling the finished dessert.

Serves 12 to 14

Crust:
   2¼ c flour
   ¾ c sugar
   ⅛ t fine sea salt
   ¾ cup (1½ sticks) unsalted butter
   2 T finely minced lemon zest
   3 T fresh lemon juice
   3 T heavy cream

Lemon curd:
   1½ c (3 sticks) unsalted butter
   2¼ c fresh lemon juice
   9 egg yolks

   3 eggs
   3 c sugar
   pinch of fine sea salt
   3 T finely minced fresh lemon zest

White chocolate lemon mousse:
   half of the lemon curd
   6 oz white chocolate, finely chopped
   2 c heavy cream
   additional lemon zest, white chocolate curls, or Candied Citrus Peel (page 97) for garnish (optional)

Prepare the crust:

Preheat oven to 350 degrees F.

In a medium bowl, mix together the flour, sugar, and salt. Cut in the butter until the mixture resembles coarse crumbs. Stir in the lemon zest and lemon juice. Add just enough heavy cream to make the dough come together in a ball without being too sticky. Press the crust mixture into a greased 12-inch tart pan with a removable bottom, or a large, deep-dish pie plate. Bake 12 to 15 minutes or until firm and done in the center. Set aside to cool.

Prepare the curd and mousse:

In a medium-size, heavy-bottomed pan or in a double boiler, melt butter with lemon juice. In a heat-resistant bowl, whisk together egg yolks, whole eggs, and sugar. Whisk about 1 cup of the hot lemon mixture into the eggs. While whisking constantly, pour the egg and lemon mixture into the pan with the remaining lemon mixture. Stir over medium-low heat until the lemon curd is thick and smooth. Do not boil.

Once the lemon curd is thick, pour it through a fine mesh strainer into a heat-resistant bowl. Stir in the zest. Prepare to make the mousse by removing half of the hot lemon curd to another bowl. Cover and chill the remaining lemon curd until ready to assemble torte. Chilling overnight is best.

Make the mousse by adding the chopped chocolate to the hot lemon curd mixture. Stir until chocolate melts. Cover and chill. Chilling overnight is best.

When mousse mixture is cold, whip the heavy cream until stiff peaks form. Fold the whipped cream into the white chocolate lemon mixture until it is light and uniform in color. Keep chilled until ready to assemble torte.

Assemble the torte:

Remove the crust to a large cake plate or platter. Mound the chilled lemon curd in the center and spread it out in a thick, even layer. Top this layer with the mousse, completely covering the edges of the lemon curd and crust. Chill or freeze. Serve right out of the refrigerator or freezer. Garnish with bits of additional lemon zest or candied lemon peel and white chocolate curls, if desired.

Multi-Berry Explosion Pie

This pie is excellent with one fruit or several. The proportions work well for a 9-inch pie. Make this when you have frozen fruit in winter, to be reminded of summer's berry bounty.

Makes one 9-inch pie; serves 8

1 baked 9-inch pie crust
1 c fresh raspberries
1 c fresh Maine blueberries
1 c fresh blackberries
1 c sliced fresh strawberries
1 c fresh black raspberries
¾ c to 1 c sugar
¼ c cornstarch
2 T cold water
2 T fresh citrus juice: lime, lemon, or orange
½ t cinnamon
whipped cream for topping

Prepare pie crust and bake (see "Baking an Unfilled Pastry Crust," page 32). Wash fruit and place in a medium-size, heavy-bottomed saucepan. Add sugar. In another bowl, dissolve cornstarch in water and citrus juice.

Cook fruit over medium heat and stir until bubbly. Stir cornstarch slurry and pour into fruit. Cook fruit until thick. Stir in cinnamon. Pour into baked crust. Cover and chill. Top with whipped cream.

Six-Apple Crisp with Fairy Butter Curls and Maple Caramel Sauce

When made with several varieties of apple, each type offers up its own texture, and special flavor.
Serves 12 to 14

6 c cored, peeled, and chopped apples
  (1 c each of six varieties)
½ c sugar
1 t cinnamon
2 T fresh lemon juice
1 c rolled oats
1 c flour
½ c brown sugar
½ c salt
1 t cinnamon
½ c cardamom
¼ t black pepper
½ c unsalted butter

Preheat oven to 375 degrees F.

Spread apples in a 4-quart baking dish. Sprinkle with sugar, cinnamon, and lemon juice. Toss to coat. In a bowl, combine rolled oats, flour, brown sugar, salt, cinnamon, cardamom, and black pepper. Add butter and cut together with a pastry blender or two knives until it is crumbly. Spread over apples.

Bake 40 minutes or until apples are tender. Serve with Maple Caramel Sauce. Top with butter curls.

Maple Caramel Sauce:
  2 c whipping cream
  ¾ c sugar
  ¼ c maple sugar
  ½ c Maine maple syrup

Combine the ingredients in heavy medium saucepan. Stir over medium heat until sugar dissolves. Increase heat and bring to boil. Reduce heat to medium-low and simmer, whisking often, for about 35 minutes, until liquid is caramel colored and reduced to 1¾ cups. Cool slightly.

This can be made three days ahead. Cover and chill. Re-warm over medium heat, stirring. Add 2 tablespoons hot water, if necessary, to dissolve any crystallized sugar.

Fairy Butter Curls:
  ½ c unsalted butter
  4 T confectioners' sugar
  1 T vanilla extract
  ¼ t salt

Cream together and scrape mixture into a zip-closure bag. Press the mixture into a long roll. With the bag open, roll it up, expelling any air from around the butter. Zip the bag closed and chill or freeze until ready to use.

To make curls: Chill a small bowl. Unwrap the chilled butter roll. Working quickly, use a vegetable peeler to gently scrape thin, curling strips of butter off the side of the roll and into the bowl. Cover and chill until ready to use.

Peach Rhubarb Cobbler with Chantilly Cream

A tad sweet and a bit sour, the flavors balance out to offer a delectable, warm, comfort-food dessert. This cobbler pairs well with Sweetgrass Winery's Peach Smash wine (see appendix).

Serves 12

Filling:
4 c peeled and sliced fresh peaches
1 c trimmed and finely chopped fresh rhubarb
juice and zest of 1 lime
1¼ c light or dark brown sugar
1 t cinnamon
1 t vanilla extract
2 T flour

Topping:
1 c flour
1 t baking powder
½ t baking soda
4 T plus 2 T light brown sugar
4 T unsalted butter, cut into small pieces
⅔ c buttermilk

Preheat oven to 425 degrees F.

Generously butter a 2-quart rectangular baking dish. Place the sliced peaches, rhubarb, lime juice, and zest in the bottom of the dish and sprinkle with the brown sugar, cinnamon, vanilla, and flour. Toss gently and spread evenly. Bake for 10 minutes.

While the fruit is baking, start on the cobbler topping. In a medium bowl, combine the flour, baking powder, baking soda, and 4 tablespoons brown sugar. Cut in the butter with a pastry cutter or two knives until it is the texture of coarse crumbs. Add buttermilk all at once and stir to form a soft dough.

Remove fruit from oven and drop generous spoonfuls of dough randomly on top. Sprinkle with the remaining 2 T of brown sugar and return to oven. Bake until fruit is bubbly and crust topping is golden brown, about 20 minutes.

Serve warm with Chantilly Cream.

Chantilly Cream:
1 c heavy cream
¼ c sugar
1 t vanilla extract

In the bowl of an electric mixer, whip the cream until soft peaks form. Sprinkle the sugar over the cream and continue beating until all the sugar is incorporated. Gently whisk in the vanilla. Continue beating only until stiff peaks form.

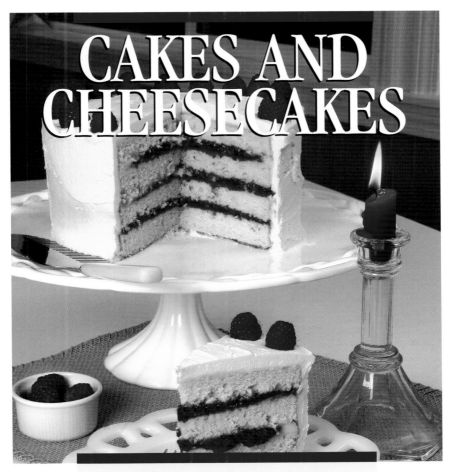

CAKES AND CHEESECAKES

The spirit of a celebration is often expressed with a cake. Light and airy or dense and rich, cakes come in all shapes and sizes. Here you will find an assortment of textures and flavors for all occasions. I like to use Swans Down or King Arthur's version of cake flour for the lightest cakes. All-purpose King Arthur white flour is my general standard for all baking—use this if you can't find "cake flour" in your local market (see appendix).

Daffodil Cake

In springtime, this cake is beautiful with a tiny vase of daffodils inserted into the center. Two batters gently layered give the appearance of a sunny daffodil suspended in a cloud.

Serves 12 to 14

White batter:

1¾ c egg whites (12 to 14 eggs)
   at room temperature
½ t fine sea salt
1½ t Bakewell Cream (see appendix) or
   cream of tartar
1½ c sugar
2 t vanilla extract
1¼ c sifted cake flour

Yellow batter:

6 egg yolks
2½ T cake flour
2½ T sugar
2 T grated lemon zest (optional)
confectioners' sugar to sprinkle on top

Preheat oven to 375 degrees F.

In the bowl of an electric mixer, beat egg whites, salt, and cream of tartar until soft peaks form. Beat in 1 cup sugar, ¼ cup at a time, beating well after each addition. Beat until stiff peaks form. Fold in vanilla until combined.

In a separate bowl, sift 1¼ cups flour with the remaining ½ cup sugar, resift four times. Sift one quarter of the flour mixture over the egg whites and fold it in gently with a rubber spatula. Repeat three more times to fold in the remaining flour mixture.

Set aside one third of this white batter in a medium bowl to be incorporated into the yellow batter.

In the bowl of an electric mixer, combine egg

yolks, cake flour, and sugar. Stir together, then turn the mixer on high speed and beat until very thick. Add lemon zest, if using. With a rubber spatula, fold this yolk mixture into reserved one third of the white batter.

Spoon yellow and white batters alternately into an ungreased 10-inch tube pan, beginning and ending with white batter. With a butter knife, cut through the batter twice to swirl the yellow batter through the white. With rubber scraper, gently smooth and even out the top.

Bake on lower oven rack 35 to 40 minutes, or until cake springs back when pressed with fingertip. Invert pan over the neck of a bottle to cool, for at least 2 hours. With an offset spatula or knife, loosen cake and gently remove from pan. Sprinkle with confectioners' sugar.

Blueberry Gingerbread

Soft gingerbread cake has long been a tradition in Maine. Enjoy this version that mingles dried apples, fresh blueberries, and three kinds of ginger.
Serves 12

2 c flour
1 t baking soda
1 t Bakewell Cream (see appendix) or
   cream of tartar
2 t ground ginger
½ t fine sea salt
1 c butter
1 T grated fresh ginger root
1¼ c brown sugar
2 T Maine maple syrup
¼ c buttermilk
½ c finely chopped dried apples
¼ c dried blueberries
2 c fresh Maine blueberries
4 T finely chopped crystallized ginger
1 c chopped pecans (optional)

Preheat the oven to 325 degrees F.

Grease a 9 by 13-inch pan.

Sift together the flour, baking soda, cream of tartar, ground ginger, and salt. Using a pastry blender or two knives, cut the butter and grated ginger into the dry ingredients until it resembles coarse crumbs. Stir in the brown sugar, maple syrup, buttermilk, dried apples, fresh blueberries, crystallized ginger, and optional pecans.

Turn into the greased pan. Smooth batter evenly. Bake 50 to 55 minutes or until a cake tester inserted in the center comes out clean. Cool 5 minutes. Cut into squares and serve warm with Maple Chantilly Cream (page 86).

Chocolate Angel Food Cake with Chocolate Whipped Cream

Angel food cake is the ultimate in (almost) guilt-free delight. This chocolate version is lovely served with a warm, dark, fudgy sauce or fresh fruit and whipped cream. For a traditional white angel food cake, substitute 1/2 cup confectioners' sugar for the cocoa powder.

Serves 12 to 14

¾ c sifted cake flour
½ c unsweetened cocoa
1¼ c sugar
1½ c egg whites (12 to 14 eggs) at room
  temperature
¼ t fine sea salt
1 t cream of tartar or Bakewell Cream
  (see appendix)
2 t vanilla extract

Preheat oven to 350 degrees F.

Sift the flour before measuring. Place the sifted flour, cocoa, and ¾ cup sugar in a bowl. Scoop the dry ingredients out of the bowl and into the sifter to sift back into the bowl. Repeat this once more.

Whisk the egg whites in a large bowl, adding salt and cream of tartar as soon as the whites become foamy. As soft peaks begin to form, add the remaining sugar and vanilla. Beat until stiff peaks form.

Using a flexible spatula, gently fold the flour mixture into the egg white mixture with a circular motion. Be sure to go all the way to the bottom of the bowl with each folding motion. Mix only until the dry ingredients are incorporated.

Gently place the batter in a 10-inch tube pan and bake immediately. Bake for 45 minutes or until the top springs back when softly pressed. Any cracks in the top of the cake should look dry.

Remove the cake from the oven and immediately invert the tube pan on the counter. (If the pan does not have legs, invert it over a wine bottle.) Cool for at least two hours.

When cake has cooled completely, run a sharp knife around the edge of the pan to loosen. Invert the cake onto a plate and remove the pan. Brush off any loose crumbs. Turn the cake right side up. Spread the chocolate whipped cream evenly over the cake. Place the frosted cake in the freezer for an hour to set the whipped cream. Serve either frozen or chilled.

Chocolate Whipped Cream:
½ c semisweet or dark chocolate bits
1 pint (2 c) heavy cream
3 T sugar, or to taste
1 t vanilla extract

Melt the chocolate in a double boiler (or microwave for one minute at high power). Stir gently until smooth. Let it cool for ten minutes until slightly warm and still liquid.

In a chilled bowl, whip the cream until soft peaks form. Sprinkle the sugar over the cream and whip another minute.

Stir one third of the whipped cream into the liquid chocolate. Very gently, fold the chocolate mixture and the vanilla extract into the remaining whipped cream.

Hidden-Veggie Cake

Carrots and zucchini add an extraordinary sweetness to this traditional cake. They are so well hidden that kids might not even notice they're there. Make it even better by using heirloom-variety carrots in a mix of colors (check your local farmers' market). Pastor Chuck's applesauce (see appendix) gives the cake a special moistness that almost eliminates the need for frosting—although my daughter Elizabeth would disagree. Cream cheese frosting is good on just about anything.

Serves 24

½ c vegetable oil
1 c applesauce
4 eggs
1½ c sugar
2 t cinnamon
1 t freshly grated nutmeg
2 c flour
2 t baking powder
1½ t baking soda
1 t fine sea salt
2 c grated fresh heirloom carrots in
    assorted colors
1 c grated fresh zucchini
½ c dried currants
½ c dried cherries
½ c chopped nuts (optional)

Preheat oven to 350 degrees F.

In a medium bowl, whisk together the oil, applesauce, eggs, and sugar. Set aside.

In a large bowl, sift together the cinnamon, nutmeg, flour, baking powder, baking soda, and salt. Stir in the grated carrots, zucchini, currants, cherries, and optional nuts. Pour the egg mixture into the dry ingredients and veggies. Stir until completely combined.

Pour the batter into an ungreased 10-inch Bundt pan or three greased 8-inch round cake pans. Set the pans on a cookie sheet and place in the oven.

Bake for 55 to 60 minutes in the Bundt pan or 35 to 40 minutes in the round cake pans. Remove from oven. Cool before removing from pan(s). (Turn the Bundt pan upside down to cool. If your Bundt pan does not have little legs to keep the top of the cake from touching the counter, carefully balance it upside down on a long-necked bottle.)

When cake is completely cool, cover with Lick-the-Bowl-Clean Coconut Cream Cheese Frosting (recipe on page 71).

Apple Butter Spice Cake with Cream Cheese Frosting

This is our family's delicious spice cake recipe. Pastor Chuck's Apple Butter (see appendix) is dark, sweet, spicy, and made here in Maine. It makes this cake will extra moist and flavorful. As an alternative to frosting, you can top it with Maple Caramel Sauce (page 43), as shown here.

Serves 12

3¾ c all-purpose flour
1 c sugar
½ t baking powder
2 t baking soda
1½ t fine sea salt
3 t cinnamon
2 t cardamom
1 t freshly grated nutmeg
6 eggs
3 c apple butter or applesauce
¾ c vegetable oil

Preheat oven to 350 degree F.

Sift the flour, sugar, baking powder, baking soda, salt, cinnamon, cardamom, and nutmeg together into a large bowl. In a separate bowl, whisk together the eggs, apple butter, and oil. Pour into the dry ingredients and stir gently until completely combined.

Grease four 9-inch round cake pans. Divide the batter evenly among the pans. Set two pans each on separate cookie sheets. Bake for 30 to 40 minutes or until a cake tester or toothpick inserted in the center comes out clean. Remove from oven and cool completely. Frost and chill or serve right away—you might have to defend the cake if hungry mouths are waiting.

Cream Cheese Frosting:

   1 c (8 oz) cream cheese
   ½ c (1 stick) butter
   ¼ t fine sea salt
   2 lb confectioners' sugar
   2 T vanilla extract
   2 to 4 T heavy cream

Cream the cream cheese and butter together with an electric mixer. Add salt. Slowly add the confectioners' sugar a couple of tablespoons at a time until it is all incorporated. Add 2 to 4 tablespoons of cream to give the frosting the consistency you like.

No Sifter? Here's a Workaround

Flour must be sifted—sometimes more than once—before using in cake recipes. If you don't have a sifter, use a wire mesh strainer and a whisk to fluff the flour before measuring. Place the flour in the strainer and use the whisk to "stir" the flour through the strainer.

Chocolate Decadence Cake

Here is an almost flourless cake. The dense center is fudgy tasting but light. There's a lot of folding going on, but it's all worth it. A cup of espresso from Portland's Coffee By Design (see appendix) complements it wonderfully.
Serves 14

6 oz bittersweet chocolate, finely chopped
2 oz unsweetened baking chocolate, finely chopped
1 c unsalted butter
½ c strong brewed coffee
6 eggs, separated, at room temperature
1 T vanilla extract
1 c dark brown sugar
½ c white sugar
⅓ c flour
confectioners' sugar to sprinkle on top

Preheat oven to 350 degrees F. Grease a 10-inch springform pan.

In a small saucepan, melt together the bittersweet and unsweetened chocolates, butter, and coffee. Cool to room temperature. Stir until completely smooth.

In the bowl of an electric mixer, beat the egg yolks, vanilla, and sugars for 6 minutes. Fold the cooled chocolate mixture into the sugar and yolks. Fold the flour into the chocolate batter.

In a clean bowl, whip the egg whites until peaks form that are firm but not dry. Gently fold the egg whites into the chocolate batter one third at a time. Pour into a springform pan. Bake until a toothpick or cake tester inserted into the center comes out with moist crumbs, about 45 minutes.

Remove from oven and cool in the pan on a rack. Run a knife around the edge of the pan and release the springform sides. Invert on a pretty plate. Carefully remove the bottom of the pan. Sprinkle with confectioners' sugar and serve.

Triple-Layer Cocoa-Dusted Espresso Mascarpone Cake

Nowhere else have I seen a version of tiramisù that climbs as high as this one. Enjoy the drama as you bring it to the table. This cake pairs well with Winterport Winery's The Flying Dutchman wine (see appendix).
Serves 14 to 16

Cake:
  4 whole eggs
  2 c sugar
  2 c flour, sifted
  ⅛ t fine sea salt
  2 t baking powder
  1 c whole milk
  4 T (½ stick) unsalted butter
  6 egg whites (use yolks in custard, below)
  1 t vanilla extract

Mascarpone custard:
  1 c plus 2 c heavy cream
  6 egg yolks
  2 egg whites

  5 T sugar
  2 t vanilla extract
  32 oz (four 8-ounce containers)
    mascarpone cheese

Espresso mixture:
  ½ c brewed espresso
  1 T sugar

Topping:
  2 T unsweetened cocoa
  2 T grated semisweet chocolate

Make the cake:

Preheat oven to 350 degrees F.

Grease and flour four 9-inch cake pans.

In the bowl of an electric mixer, beat the four whole eggs until light and fluffy, a pale yellow color, and tripled in volume—about 5 minutes. Add sugar, a tablespoon at a time, and continue beating the mixture for about 3 minutes.

Sift the flour, salt, and baking powder together in a small bowl. Add the flour mixture slowly to the eggs. Beat the mixture just until smooth.

Heat the milk and the butter over low heat in a small saucepan, stirring. Bring barely to a boil. Remove from heat. Beat into the flour and egg mixture. Stir in the vanilla.

In a clean bowl, whip the egg whites until stiff peaks form. Fold gently into batter until well combined. Pour the batter into the prepared cake pans.

Bake 14 to 16 minutes. Check with a cake tester inserted into the center. If it comes out clean, remove the cakes from the oven. If not, check every two minutes until done. Cool for about 5 minutes in the pan, then remove the cakes from the pans and cool on a wire rack. Wrap in plastic until ready to use.

Make the mascarpone custard:

Heat 1 cup heavy cream in a small, heavy-bottomed saucepan over low heat until bubbles form around the edge. Whisk the yolks together in a medium bowl. Whisking constantly, pour half of the hot cream into the eggs, then pour the egg mixture back into the saucepan over low heat until thick, stirring all the time.

Wash and dry the medium bowl. Strain the cooked cream mixture through a fine mesh sieve into the bowl. Cover and chill.

In the bowl of an electric mixer, beat 2 egg whites until soft peaks form. Add 2 tablespoons sugar and 2 teaspoons vanilla and beat until stiff peaks form. Set aside.

In a separate bowl, whip 2 cups heavy cream. Add the 3 tablespoons sugar as soon as soft peaks form. Continue whipping until stiff peaks form.

In a large bowl, gently whisk the mascarpone cheese until it has softened. Then it's time to fold everything together. Gently stir in the chilled custard. Fold in the whipped egg whites. Fold in the whipped cream until completely combined and still very light.

Make the espresso mixture:

In a small bowl, whisk the warm espresso and sugar together. When the sugar is dissolved, you are read to begin assembling your cake.

Assemble the cake:

Place the cakes on a cutting board. Trim so the tops are flat. Brush off any crumbs. Place one layer of cake on a pretty platter or cake stand. Paint the top of the cake with the espresso mixture, using a soft bristle or silicone pastry brush. Place ½ cup to ¾ cup of the mascarpone custard on top and smooth evenly. Place another layer of cake on top and repeat with the espresso and mascarpone custard. Continue until all four are evenly layered, one on top of the other.

Use the remaining mascarpone custard to frost the outside of the cake, covering it entirely. Dust the top with cocoa and grated chocolate. Chill.

Serve very cold. Slice thinly with a serrated knife.

A Delicate Dusting for Cakes

When you don't want to cover a cake with rich frosting, a simple sifting of confectioners' sugar or cocoa powder is all you need for an elegant finish. A paper doily makes an instant stencil. Set it atop the cake, and then sprinkle with confectioners' sugar or cocoa. Carefully lift the doily straight up and off the cake to reveal a lovely design. Do this just before serving the cake.

Chocolate "WOW" Cake

Here is a majestic, never-fail chocolate cake recipe that is sure to please a crowd. The combination of cream cheese and butter makes it very rich. The chocolates create a velvety, dark, rich texture. This recipe is best made in its entirety even though it makes a lot of cake! The baked cakes freeze well and retain their moistness.

Serves 16 to 18

2 c butter
1 c (8 oz) cream cheese
2 c sugar
9 eggs
4½ c flour
5 T unsweetened cocoa
1 t fine sea salt
1½ T baking powder
1 c milk or buttermilk
3 T vanilla extract
18 oz bittersweet chocolate
2 oz unsweetened baking chocolate

Preheat oven to 350 degrees F.

Cream the butter, cream cheese, and sugar. Add eggs one at a time, incorporating completely after each addition.

Sift together flour, cocoa, salt, and baking powder.

In a measuring cup, mix milk and vanilla together.

Melt bittersweet and unsweetened chocolates together. This is best done in a double boiler. Stir the melted chocolates until they are combined.

Add the dry ingredients, milk mixture, and melted chocolate alternately to the creamed butter and eggs. Beat until all are incorporated into a beautiful, velvety chocolate batter.

This recipe is versatile. It will make enough for four 8-inch round cake pans, or a 9 by 13-inch pan and 24 cupcakes, or a 12-inch springform pan plus another small pan.

Bake cakes just until a cake tester comes out clean with moist crumbs. Plan to bake cupcakes 20 to 25 minutes; 8-inch rounds 30 to 35 minutes; and a 12-inch springform pan at least 45 minutes. Do not over bake.

Frost with Whipped Ganache (page 68).

White Chocolate Raspberry Lily Cake

I invented this dessert for a baby shower celebration for a dear friend—and Olivia, the "baby," is now almost twelve. It has a bunch of easy steps that create a whole that is much more than the sum of its parts—a beautiful combination of crimson and white, sweet and fruity. Use the freshest organic eggs and pure vanilla for the best flavor. The cake layers can be baked a day ahead and wrapped well or stored in an airtight container until you are ready to assemble the layers. Sweetgrass Winery's Beaujolais pairs well with this cake (see appendix).

Serves 14 to 16

Cake:
10 egg whites
½ c plus ¾ c sugar
1 c butter, plus 2 T for greasing the pan
1 t vanilla extract
3 c flour
1 T baking powder
1 t fine sea salt
1 c buttermilk

White chocolate ganache:
12 oz white chocolate, finely chopped
½ c heavy cream

Chantilly cream:
1 c heavy cream
¼ c sugar
1 t vanilla extract

White chocolate buttercream:

1 c unsalted butter at room temperature
1 c White Chocolate Ganache (see above)
1 T vanilla extract
1 c Chantilly Cream (see above)
2 lb confectioners' sugar
¼ t fine sea salt

Raspberry coulis:

1 pint (2 c) fresh or frozen raspberries
½ c sugar

Make the cakes:

Preheat oven to 350 degrees F.

Grease two 9 by 13-inch pans with butter. In the bowl of an electric mixer, whip the egg whites until soft peaks form. Turn the mixer down to a slow setting and sprinkle in ½ cup of sugar, a teaspoon at a time, until it is completely incorporated. Whip the mixture on high until stiff peaks form and set it aside.

In another bowl, cream the butter, ¾ cup sugar, and vanilla, with the mixer set to a medium-high setting for 10 minutes. This step makes the cake very light and fluffy.

In another bowl, sift together the flour, baking powder, and salt. Slowly mix the flour mixture and the buttermilk into the fluffy butter mixture, alternating between the dry and wet ingredients. Scrape down the sides of the bowl and mix just until completely incorporated. Stir a heaping cup of the beaten egg whites into the batter. Gently fold the remaining egg whites into the batter using a spatula. Divide the batter equally between the two pans, spreading it into an even layer.

Bake for 25 to 30 minutes or until the center springs back when you touch it and a cake tester comes out clean. Remove from pans and cool completely.

Make the white chocolate ganache:

In a double boiler, stir the white chocolate and cream over medium heat until the chocolate is smooth and melted. Cool to room temperature.

Make the Chantilly cream:

In the bowl of an electric mixer, whip the heavy cream until soft peaks form. Sprinkle the sugar over the cream and continue whipping until all the sugar is incorporated. Gently whip in the vanilla. Continue whipping only until stiff peaks form.

Make white chocolate buttercream:

Cream the butter in the bowl of an electric mixer for 5 minutes, scraping down the sides often, until it is light and fluffy. Add 1 cup of the cooled white chocolate ganache and the vanilla, and whisk another 5 minutes. Add 1 cup of the Chantilly cream and whisk again. Slowly add the confectioners' sugar a tablespoon at a time until completely incorporated. Add the sea salt.

Make the raspberry coulis:

In a small saucepan, stir together the raspberries and sugar. Stir over medium heat until the sugar has completely dissolved and the berries have broken down. Strain the raspberry mixture through a sieve into a bowl, pressing on the pulp to extract all the juice. Discard the seeds.

Assemble the cake:

If the tops of the cake layers have domed while baking, trim with a serrated knife to create flat surfaces. Cut each layer in half horizontally. Place the first cake layer on a large platter. Brush off any stray crumbs. Spread a thin layer of white chocolate ganache over the top.

Spread a layer of Chantilly cream over the ganache, creating a ½-inch-high rim of Chantilly cream all around the edge of the cake.

Gently spoon one quarter of the raspberry coulis onto the center of the first layer, spreading it out to the edge. The rim of Chantilly cream will serve as a barrier so the coulis doesn't run down the sides.

Carefully set the second layer of cake on top of the coulis. Press gently to set the cake, but not enough to squish the Chantilly cream out of the center. Repeat layers of Chantilly cream and coulis and apply third cake layer. Repeat. Spread the top of the fourth layer with white chocolate ganache.

Frost the entire cake with the white chocolate buttercream. Be sure to cover every bit of the sides and top.

Garnish with fresh raspberries as shown or decorate with coulis and buttercream: Place the remaining coulis into a pastry bag fitted with a small tip. Place the remaining white chocolate ganache in another pastry bag fitted with a small tip. (If you don't have pastry bags, you can use sturdy plastic freezer bags. Place the coulis or ganache inside, seal the top, then snip off one of the bottom corners.) Alternately drizzle the coulis and pipe the ganache in a design of your choice or in random patterns all over the top and sides of the cake. Chill until ready to serve.

Hot Fudge Pudding Cake

This recipe is magic. You spread the batter in the pan, sprinkle it with sugar, and pour water over the top. Presto, change-o! A few oven-baked minutes later, you have a pudding-like cake that has its own sauce on the bottom. Top with vanilla or coffee ice cream for an even richer dessert.

Makes 9 servings

1 c flour
2 t baking powder
¾ c sugar
¼ t salt
3 T plus ¼ c unsweetened cocoa powder
½ c buttermilk
2 T vegetable oil
1 c brown sugar, firmly packed
1¾ c hot water
heavy cream for garnish

Preheat oven to 350 degrees F.

Grease a 9 by 9-inch baking pan. In a large bowl, stir together flour, baking powder, sugar, salt, and 3 tablespoons cocoa. Add buttermilk and oil. Stir until combined. Spread evenly in pan.

In a small bowl, blend the brown sugar and ¼ cup cocoa. Sprinkle this mixture evenly over the batter in the pan. Pour the hot water over all. Do not stir. Bake 45 minutes. Serve warm or cold, drizzled with heavy cream.

Red Velvet Beet Cake Studded with Dark Chocolate

This one-bowl red velvet cake takes its color from cooked beets instead of food coloring. One-bowl cakes are the easiest to make because all of the ingredients are stirred up at once to create a moist, smooth batter. Cover it with a creamy, luscious frosting such as Whipped Ganache (page 68) or Cream Cheese Frosting (page 57).

Serves 16

2½ c flour
2 c sugar
1 c buttermilk
1 t baking soda
1 t fine sea salt
1 c vegetable oil
1 c cooked puréed beets
3 eggs
¼ c unsweetened cocoa
1 T white vinegar
frosting recipe of your choice
dark chocolate bits or shaved chocolate
   for garnish

Preheat oven to 300 degrees F.

Grease and flour two 9-inch cake pans.

Place all ingredients except frosting and dark chocolate bits in a large bowl. Whisk until completely combined. Divide evenly between the two pans. Bake 40 to 50 minutes until a cake tester inserted in the center comes out with moist crumbs. Cool. Remove from pans. Assemble the layers and cover with frosting of your choice. Garnish with chocolate bits or shavings.

Molten Chocolate Lava Cakes with Espresso Cream

Enjoy these liquid-centered cakes right out of the oven. The melted chocolate middles are hot and soft, perfect for a cold winter's night. This cake pairs well with Coffee By Design's Costa Rica Tarrazu La Minita Estate blend (see appendix). *NOTE:* Batter requires a minimum one-hour chill time before baking.

Serves 8

Cakes:

- 1 c all-purpose flour
- ¾ c unsweetened cocoa powder
- 3 T instant espresso powder
- 1½ t baking powder
- 1 c (2 sticks) unsalted butter, melted
- 1½ c light brown sugar
- 1 c melted bittersweet chocolate
- 4 eggs
- 3 T brewed espresso
- 2 t vanilla extract
- 16 T (1 c) semisweet chocolate chips

Espresso Cream:

- 1 c chilled whipping cream
- 3 T confectioners' sugar
- 2 t instant espresso powder

In a medium bowl, sift flour, cocoa, espresso powder, and baking powder. In a large bowl, whisk butter, brown sugar, and melted chocolate until completely combined. Whisk in eggs one at a time. Mix in brewed espresso and vanilla. Whisk in dry ingredients all at once.

Grease eight 1-cup ovenproof mugs or ramekins. Divide batter among the eight mugs, placing about ⅔ cup in each. Place 2 tablespoons of chocolate chips on each. Gently press chips into the center of the batter. Cover and refrigerate mugs at least 1 hour or overnight.

Position rack in center of oven and preheat to 350 degrees F. Remove mugs from refrigerator and let stand at room temperature 10 minutes. Bake uncovered until cakes are puffed and crusty and a cake tester inserted into the center comes out with thick batter attached, about 25 minutes.

Let cakes cool while you whip the cream, about 5 minutes. NOTE: Whipped cream also can be prepared up to one hour ahead and kept chilled.

To prepare the whipped cream, combine the cream, confectioners' sugar, and espresso powder in a medium bowl. Whip until stiff peaks form. Top the hot cakes with the whipped cream and serve.

Traditional Christmas Eve Cheesecake

A cheesecake with a graham-cracker crust and topped with cherries was on the table every Christmas Eve as far back as I can remember. This recipe started out as Mom's, and she taught me how to make it when I was five years old. Then, as I grew, I made it my own. I hope it brings you as much joy as it has brought me. Cellardoor Vineyard's Queen Anne's Lace wine pairs well with this cheesecake (see appendix).

Serves 12

Crust:

1 c finely crumbled graham crackers
2 T sugar
½ t cinnamon
8 T (1 stick) melted butter

Filling:

4 c (four 8-oz packages) cream cheese
1 c sugar
4 eggs
1 t vanilla extract, or more to taste
1 t fresh lemon juice

Stir the graham cracker crumbs, sugar, cinnamon, and melted butter together in a bowl. Once the crumbs are well moistened, press the entire mixture into a well-greased 9-inch or 10-inch springform pan. (Be sure the pan bottom is properly set and secure.) Press down the moist crumbs evenly across the bottom of the pan and an inch or so up the sides, making sure the seam around the edge of the base is completely covered with crust. Set the springform pan on a sheet pan with sides at least ½ inch high. This protects your oven from leaky springform accidents.

Preheat oven to 325 degrees F.

Cream the cheese and sugar together in the bowl of an electric mixer. Scrape down the sides often to be sure the mixture is smooth and creamy. Add the eggs one at a time, beating after each addition. Add the vanilla and lemon juice. Stir until combined.

At this point you can decide whether you want a dense or light cake. For a dense cake, stop mixing now. For a very light cake, turn your mixer up to high and beat the batter for 10 minutes more. Pour the batter into the crust and gently smooth the top.

Bake the cake for 40 minutes. Turn off the heat and let the cake sit in the oven for 15 minutes. Remove from the oven, cover, and chill.

When you're ready to serve, run a knife around the inside of the pan, all the way down to the bottom, pressing right up against the side. Release the springform hinge and remove the sides. If the cake is cold enough, you can carefully run an offset spatula under the bottom crust and slide the entire cake onto a platter or cake stand. If the cake is not completely cool, you might want to leave it on the bottom of the springform pan and place that on your platter or cake stand.

Top with cherries, blueberries, hot fudge, or other topping of your choice.

Fresh Berry Swirl Cheesecake

This cheesecake pairs well with Sweetgrass Winery's Cranberry Smash wine (see appendix).

Serves 12

Crust:
- 1 c finely crumbled gingersnap cookies
- 2 T sugar
- ½ t cinnamon
- 8 T (1 stick) butter, melted

Filling:
- 4 c (four 8-ounce packages) cream cheese
- 1 c sugar
- 4 eggs
- 1 t vanilla extract
- 1 t fresh lemon juice
- 1 cup puréed berries of your choice
  (about 1½ c whole berries)

Prepare crust as described in the instructions for Traditional Christmas Eve Cheesecake (page 60), but use crumbled gingersnap cookies in place of the graham crackers.

Purée 1½ cups fresh berries (yields 1 cup purée) and set aside.

Prepare the filling as described in the Traditional Christmas Eve Cheesecake recipe, but *remove 1 cup of filling* from the bowl before pouring the rest into the crust. Blend the puréed fresh berries with the reserved filling and pour onto the plain batter already in the crust. Using a knife, swirl the berry batter into the plain batter just until it is barely distributed.

Bake as directed in the traditional Christmas Eve Cheesecake recipe.

Marble Cheesecake

Crust:
- 1 c finely crumbled graham crackers
- 2 T sugar
- ½ t cinnamon (optional)
- 8 T (1 stick) butter, melted

Filling:
- 4 c (four 8-ounce packages) cream cheese
- 1 c sugar
- 4 eggs
- 1 t vanilla extract
- 1 c chopped semisweet chocolate

Prepare crust as described in the instructions for Traditional Christmas Eve Cheesecake (page 60), deleting the cinnamon, if you wish.

Melt chocolate over hot water in the top of a double boiler. Set aside to cool to room temperature.

Prepare filling as described in the Traditional Christmas Eve Cheesecake recipe, but *remove 1 cup of filling* from the bowl before pouring the rest into the crust. Blend the melted chocolate into the reserved filling and pour onto the plain batter already in the crust. Using a knife, swirl the chocolate batter into the plain batter just until it is barely distributed.

Bake as directed in the Traditional Christmas Eve Cheesecake recipe. Serve topped with Hot Fudge Sauce (page 90).

Pumpkin Cheesecake with Maple Caramel Sauce

Pumpkin adds moistness and flavor to this creamy cheesecake. Take the extra time to beat the batter to a mousselike consistency. This dessert pairs well with Winterport Winery's sparkling Back Porch Cider (see appendix).
Serves 12

Crust:
  1 c finely crumbled gingersnap cookies
  2 T sugar
  ½ t cinnamon
  8 T (1 stick) butter, melted

Filling:
  2 c (two 8-oz packages) cream cheese
  2 c cooked, puréed pumpkin
  1 c sugar
  1 t cinnamon

½ t ground ginger
¼ t ground nutmeg
4 eggs
1 t vanilla extract
1 t fresh lemon juice

Prepare crust and filling as described in the instructions for Traditional Christmas Eve Cheesecake (page 60) Serve drizzled with the same Maple Caramel Sauce used in the Six-Apple Crisp recipe (page 43).

Lemon Curd Topping for Cheesecake

Sweet and tart, this lemon curd tops tradi-tional cheesecake, adding another texture to the light, cheesy base.

Makes about 2½ cups

4 lemons
6 egg yolks
6 T unsalted butter
1¼ cup sugar

Wash the lemons. Zest them to collect ¼ cup of zest. Then juice them to collect 1 cup of juice. In a small bowl, whisk half of the juice into the egg yolks.

Place the other half cup of juice, zest, butter, and sugar in a heavy-bottomed saucepan on low heat. Whisk constantly until the sugar is dissolved. Remove from heat.

Add ½ cup of the hot mixture to the egg yolks, whisking constantly. Return the warmed eggs to the saucepan, whisking constantly. Heat this mixture gently until thick, but do not boil or it will separate.

Strain through a fine mesh sieve. Pour into a clean, hot jar. Cover and chill until ready to use. Serve by spreading over the cooked, cooled cheesecake after removing it from pan, then decorate with fruit of your choice

Quadruple Chocolate Cheesecake

This recipe was developed for catering. It is dark, dense, delicious, and very rich, so slice into small servings. Tried and true, it consistently pleases a crowd. This cheesecake pairs well with Winterport Winery's Raspberry Rain wine (see appendix).

Serves 24

Crust:

1 c finely crumbled chocolate wafer cookies or chocolate graham crackers
2 T sugar
1 T unsweetened cocoa
8 T (1 stick) butter, melted

Filling:

3 c (three 8-oz packages) cream cheese
1 c sugar
6 T Dutch process cocoa
4 eggs
1 T vanilla extract
2 lb bittersweet chocolate
2 oz unsweetened baking chocolate
1 c sour cream
2 T unsalted butter, softened

Combine the bittersweet and unsweetened chocolate and melt in a double boiler. Remove from heat and cool to room temperature. It will stay liquidy until it cools.

Stir the cookie crumbs, sugar, cocoa, and melted butter together in a bowl. Once the crumbs are well moistened, place the entire mixture into a well-greased 10-inch springform pan. (Be sure the pan bottom is properly set and secure.) Press down the moist crumbs evenly across the bottom of the pan and an inch or so up the sides, making sure the seam around the edge of the base is completely covered with crust. Set the springform pan on a sheet pan with sides at least ½ inch high. This protects your oven from leaky-springform accidents.

Preheat oven to 350 degrees F.

Cream the cream cheese, sugar, and cocoa together in the bowl of an electric mixer. Scrape down the sides often to be sure the mixture is smooth and creamy. Add the eggs one at a time, beating after each addition. Add the vanilla and stir. Add the melted, cooled chocolate, sour cream, and butter. Beat until smooth and completely uniform in color.

At this point you can decide whether you want a dense or light cake. For a dense cake, stop mixing now. For a very light cake, turn your mixer up to high and beat the batter for 10 minutes more. Pour the batter into the crust and gently smooth the top.

Bake the cake for 10 minutes at 350 degrees. Lower the heat to 325 and bake another 35 minutes. Remove cake from the oven and cool in the pan. Chill 4 hours or overnight. This cake keeps well for up to three days before serving.

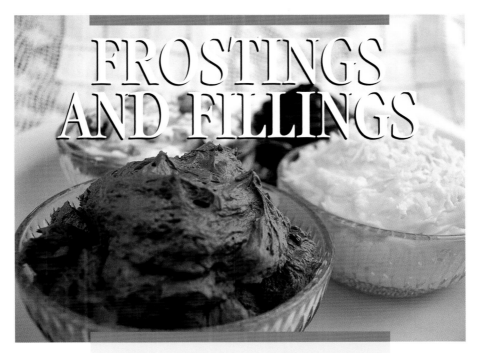

FROSTINGS AND FILLINGS

Have no fear, the frosting is here! This is the sweet stuff that makes our cakes come together. There are times, too many to mention, that a cake reaches its full potential because of the frosting that covers it. Fillings are a hidden element that adds a surprise to the center of your dessert. Most frostings and fillings are interchangeable.

Sweet and Simple Butter Cream Frosting

Since confectioners' sugar, butter, and vanilla are staples of the pantry, this recipe can come together quickly and without a trip to the market. Variations are as simple as adding a bit of this or a dash of that.

Makes enough to frost and fill an 8-inch 3-layer cake

Basic Butter Cream Frosting:

12 T (¾ c) soft unsalted butter
6 to 8 T light cream
1 T vanilla extract
½ t salt
6 c confectioners' sugar
food coloring (optional)

In a large bowl or the bowl of an electric mixer, beat together the butter, cream, and vanilla until smooth and light, about 5 minutes. Mixing at slow speed, add the salt and confectioners' sugar. Beat until smooth, adding more confectioners' sugar or cream until you achieve the desired spreadable consistency. Scrape down the sides of the bowl and beat again until very light and fluffy. Add food coloring of your choice for decorating cupcakes and cookies.

Variations:

Milk Chocolate: Melt ½ cup chocolate bits and allow to cool before adding to the frosting mixture

Dark Chocolate: Melt ½ cup chocolate bits and allow to cool. Stir cooled chocolate and ½ cup unsweetened cocoa powder into the frosting mixture.

Mint: Add 1 teaspoon peppermint extract.

Lemon: Add 3 tablespoons fresh lemon juice.

Strawberry: Add ¼ cup crushed strawberries.

Orange: Add 2 tablespoons frozen orange juice concentrate.

Blueberry: Add 2 tablespoons blueberry jam.

Superb Vanilla: Add 2 tablespoons mascarpone cheese and 1 tablespoon vanilla extract.

Cinnamon: Add 2 teaspoons cinnamon.

Harvest Maple: Add 1 teaspoon cinnamon, ½ teaspoon nutmeg, ¼ teaspoon cardamom, and 2 tablespoons maple syrup or maple sugar.

Ultra Light: Using any of these variations, whip 1 cup of heavy cream until stiff peaks form. Fold the whipped cream into the completed frosting.

Creamy Sweet and Tangy Frosting

S lightly tangy, this cream-cheesy frosting is great on flavorful cakes.

Makes enough to frost and fill an 8- or 9-inch 2-layer cake

1 c milk
1 c heavy cream
pinch of salt
½ c flour
3 T water
2 c sugar
1 c unsalted butter
1 c (8 oz pkg) cream cheese
1 T vanilla extract

Heat the milk, cream, and salt in a heavy-bottomed saucepan until bubbles form around the edges. Stir together the flour and water to make a slurry. Stir the slurry into the hot milk. Whisk constantly over medium heat until mixture thickens. Pour through a fine mesh strainer into a container. Discard any lumps. Cover and chill thickened milk.

Cream the sugar, butter, cream cheese, and vanilla. Scrape down the sides of the bowl. Beat until very light and fluffy. Add the cold thickened milk. Beat five minutes, scraping down the sides of the bowl often.

Chocolate Paste

A n outstanding not-too-sweet dairy-free filling for cakes. Whip and fold in 2 cups of heavy cream to make a luscious pie filling or mousse-like dessert.

Makes 4 cups

1¼ c water
1¼ c sugar
2 c Dutch process cocoa

Place water and sugar in a medium saucepan. Stir together and bring to a boil. Whisk in cocoa. Continue stirring and boiling until the mixture has thickened. Strain into a heat-resistant container. Cover with plastic wrap and chill.

Chocolate Ganache

When warm, ganache is thick and spreadable. When cooled, it is wonderful as the center of chocolate truffles. For a sweeter result, omit the unsweetened baking chocolate.

Makes enough to frost and fill an 8- or 9-inch 2-layer cake

Dark or milk chocolate version:
- 1 lb excellent quality dark or milk chocolate, finely chopped
- 1 oz unsweetened baking chocolate, finely chopped
- 2 c heavy cream

White chocolate version:
- 1 lb excellent quality white chocolate, finely chopped
- 2 c heavy cream

Place the chopped chocolate in a heat-resistant bowl. Heat the heavy cream until very hot but not boiling. Pour the hot cream over the chocolate. Let sit for three minutes, then stir until smooth and satiny. Spread warm ganache on cake, serve warm with sliced fruit.

Whipped Ganache:
Pour warm ganache into the bowl of an electric mixer, cover, and cool to room temperature. When cool, whip for 5 minutes. The color will lighten and the ganache will become fluffy and frostinglike.

Peanut Butter Frosting

Try this on chocolate cake with a chocolate fudge sauce drizzled over the top.
Makes enough to frost and fill an 8- or 9-inch 2-layer cake

2 c creamy peanut butter
1 c unsalted butter, softened
3 c confectioners' sugar
2 t vanilla extract
½ t salt
1 to 2 T cream or water, as needed

Place all ingredients, with the exception of the cream or water, in the bowl of an electric mixer. Beat together until creamy. Scrape down the bowl. Beat the filling for 6 minutes on high until the mixture is fluffy and light. Thin with a tablespoon or two of cream or water if necessary to achieve desired consistency.

Cloud Nine Cooked Frosting

The cooked and cooled milk in this frosting gives the finished product a light, silky feel on your tongue. Use it to frost any cake.
Makes enough to frost and fill a 9-inch 3-layer cake

1 c milk
1 c heavy cream
pinch of salt
½ c flour
3 T water
2 c sugar
1 c unsalted butter
½ c vegetable shortening
1 T vanilla extract

Heat the milk and cream in a heavy-bottomed saucepan until bubbles form around the edges. Stir together the salt, flour, and water to make a slurry. Stir the slurry into the hot milk. Whisk constantly over medium heat until mixture thickens. Pour through a fine mesh strainer into a container. Discard any lumps. Cover and chill.

Cream sugar, butter, shortening, and vanilla. Scrape down the sides of the bowl. Beat until very light and fluffy. Add the cold thickened milk. Beat for 5 minutes, scraping down the sides of the bowl often.

Caramel Filling

Real, honest-to-goodness caramel whisked together with tangy cream cheese and pure vanilla—absolutely divine.

Makes enough to fill two 8- or 9-inch 3-layer cakes

1 c (8 oz) cream cheese at room temperature
¾ c whipping cream
1 T vanilla extract
2¼ c sugar
⅔ c water
9 T butter at room temperature

Whisk together cream cheese, cream, and vanilla in a small bowl until smooth. Place sugar and water in a large, heavy-bottomed saucepan over medium-low heat, stirring constantly, 6 minutes or until sugar dissolves. Increase heat to high. Bring syrup to a boil without stirring. Using a silicone or bristle pastry brush dipped in hot water, wash down any sugar crystals that form on the side of the pan. Cook without stirring, 10 minutes or just until syrup turns a deep amber color. Whisk in butter, a tablespoon at a time. Gradually whisk in cream cheese mixture until smooth. Remove from heat. Cool 10 minutes, whisking occasionally. Cool before using.

Cooked Vanilla Frosting

This is an old-fashioned cooked frosting. Heat it gently and whip it for a long time. Your reward will be a satiny, sweet topping for your favorite cake.

Makes enough to frost and fill an 8-inch 2-layer cake

1 c sugar
½ t Bakewell Cream (see appendix) or cream of tartar
3 egg whites
¼ c water
1 T vanilla extract

Combine all the ingredients in a double boiler. Whisk gently for about 4 minutes or until the sugar dissolves. Pour into the bowl of an electric mixer and beat on high for about 8 minutes.

Lick-the-Bowl-Clean Coconut Cream Cheese Frosting

When my daughter Elizabeth makes this frosting, she licks the bowl and beaters so clean that I have to check twice to make sure they get washed.

Makes enough to frost and fill an 8- or 9-inch 2-layer cake

½ c unsalted butter
8 oz cream cheese
1½ lb confectioners' sugar
1 T vanilla extract
2 T heavy cream
1½ c shredded coconut

Cream the butter and cream cheese together. Scrape down the bowl often. Slowly incorporate the confectioners' sugar. Add the vanilla and heavy cream. Whip the frosting for 4 minutes. If the mixture is too dense, add another tablespoon of cream. If the mixture is too runny, add more confectioners' sugar, 1 tablespoon at a time. When you have the consistency you want, stir in the coconut. Use immediately or chill until needed.

White Chocolate Frosting

One morning I woke up thinking about what to bring as a treat to share at our local swing dance. I decided to make an applesauce cake. I had a banana that was ripe and ready, so I threw it in the batter. The cake was so moist and lovely! I wanted to top it with a cream cheese frosting, but there wasn't a bag of confectioners' sugar to be found. This was what I came up with. My dancing pals loved it!

Makes enough to frost and fill an 8- or 9-inch 2-layer cake

8 oz white chocolate bits
½ c half and half or light cream
2 c (16 oz) cream cheese or Neufchâtel cheese
   (a lower-fat version)
¾ c brown sugar
¼ t salt
2 t vanilla extract
2 T maple sugar

Melt the white chocolate with the cream in a double boiler. When the bits are completely melted, stir until you have a beautiful, smooth ganache. Let this cool for a few minutes.

In the bowl of an electric mixer, whip the cream cheese and brown sugar until the mixture is light and fluffy, scraping down the sides of the bowl so there are no lumpy bits of cream cheese left—about 4 minutes. Slowly add the ganache to the cream cheese a spoonful at a time. When the mixture has been completely incorporated, add the salt, vanilla, and maple sugar. Whisk again for another 3 or 4 minutes, scraping the sides of the bowl often. Taste and add more sugar if necessary.

Maple Walnut Butter Frosting

My mom always ordered maple walnut ice cream when we went out for a frozen treat. Here is a nod to her favorite flavor. *Makes enough to frost or fill an 8- or 9-inch 3-layer cake*

½ c unsalted butter
1 c (8 oz) cream cheese
1½ lb confectioners' sugar
1 T vanilla extract
2 T heavy cream
1½ c shredded coconut

In the bowl of an electric mixer, cream the butter and cream cheese together. Scrape down the bowl often. Slowly incorporate the confectioners' sugar. Add the vanilla and heavy cream. Whip the frosting for 4 minutes. If the mixture is too dense, add another tablespoon of cream. If the mixture is too runny, add more confectioners' sugar, 1 tablespoon at a time. When you have the consistency you want, stir in the coconut. Use immediately or chill until needed.

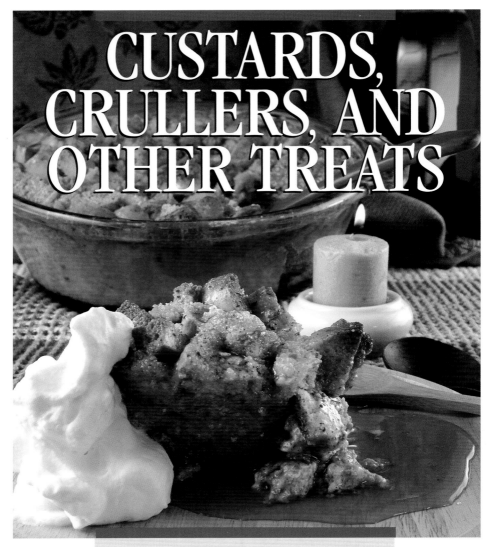

CUSTARDS, CRULLERS, AND OTHER TREATS

So many desserts. So little time. Here are a few that belong in a category of their own. Whether you are looking for a special occasion dazzler or simple, family night comfort food, you'll find it here.

Cream Puffs or Éclairs with Custard Filling

Little cream puffs or long éclairs come from this same dough. The batter puffs up in the oven and creates a crisp shell with a moist cavity inside. This custard is easy and delicious. It's one of my favorite dessert elements of all time. The recipe doubles well.

Makes 20 large éclairs or cream puffs

1 c water
¼ t salt
½ c butter
1 c flour
4 eggs

Preheat oven to 400 degrees F.

In a medium saucepan bring the water, salt, and butter to a boil. Remove from heat and stir in flour all at once with a wooden spoon. Return to low heat and stir until mixture forms a ball and leaves the side of the pan, about three minutes.

Remove from heat and pour into a heat-resistant bowl. Add eggs one at a time, beating vigorously after each addition until the mixture is smooth and glossy.

Place dough in a pastry bag and pipe golf ball-sized puffs two inches apart on a parchment-lined sheet pan. Bake 40 to 50 minutes or until golden but not brown. (The puffs can be made in any size you like, with suitable adjustments to baking time.) Remove from oven and cool on a wire rack.

To serve, cut or break in half and fill with custard or ice cream, and top with crushed fruit or melted chocolate.

Unfilled, the cooled, baked puffs freeze well in a sealed container or plastic bag.

Custard Filling:
1½ c whole milk
¼ c sugar
1 T cornstarch
pinch of salt
2 egg yolks
1 t (or more, to taste) vanilla extract

Slowly heat milk in a small, heavy saucepan, just until bubbles form around the edge. In a bowl, combine sugar, cornstarch, and salt. Stir to mix well. Whisk into hot milk all at once. Continue heating and whisking until the milk comes to a boil. Reduce heat and simmer 1 minute.

Whisk the egg yolks in a medium size bowl. Whisk ½ cup of the hot thickened milk into the egg yolks. Whisking all the time, return this mixture to the pan. Continue to stir over low heat until the custard thickens and bubbles. Stir in vanilla and salt. Pour into a heat-resistant bowl. Cover and chill.

French Crullers

My earliest recollection about these fried cakes—sometimes called beignets—is of a family visit to a sugar house deep in the woods. I had just learned that it takes 40 gallons of sap to make a gallon of maple syrup and proudly announced this to the gentleman stirring the bubbling sap in an enormous iron kettle much larger than my five-year-old self. He was so impressed that he took me inside to enjoy fresh crullers, hot from the fryer. I topped them with a splash of fresh syrup, savoring each luscious drop.

Serves 6 to 8

2 T sugar
½ t salt
¼ c butter
1 c water
1¼ c flour
4 eggs
1 t vanilla extract
vegetable shortening for frying

Combine the sugar, salt, butter, and water in a saucepan. Bring to a boil. Remove from heat and stir in the flour all at once. Return to heat and stir until the mixture forms a ball.

There are two ways to add the eggs. If you have a strong arm, you can mix them by hand. Remove the pan from heat and add the eggs one at a time. You must mix them in quickly to avoid ending up with scrambled eggs in your dough. Alternatively, you can place the hot dough in the bowl of an electric mixer. Add the eggs one at a time and beat until completely incorporated. Either way, be sure the eggs are all mixed in and you have a smooth, glossy dough. Add vanilla and stir.

Fill a pan or deep fryer about halfway with vegetable shortening and turn on medium heat. When the shortening is melted and reaches 365 degrees F, you can start frying.

Place your dough into a pastry bag fitted with a large tip or no tip at all. Carefully press out 4 to 6 inches of dough into the hot fat. Cook until light golden brown on both sides. Remove with tongs or a slotted spoon to a baking sheet or platter lined with paper towels. Continue cooking until all the batter is used.

Sprinkle with cinnamon sugar or vanilla sugar, or drizzle with maple syrup for an extra burst of flavor.

Old-Fashioned Doughnuts with Cinnamon Sugar

To make apple doughnuts, substitute Pastor Chuck's Apple Butter (see appendix) for the butter to make apple doughtnuts.

Makes 2 dozen

3 eggs
1 c sugar
4 T butter, softened
4 c flour
4 t baking powder
1 t baking soda
1 t salt
¾ t freshly ground nutmeg
⅔ c buttermilk
1 t vanilla extract
vegetable shortening for frying
1 c sugar
2 T cinnamon

In a large bowl, beat the eggs and sugar until light and fluffy. Mix in the butter. Sift together the flour, baking powder, baking soda, salt, and nutmeg, and add gradually to egg mixture. Add the buttermilk and vanilla. Stir until the mixture is smooth. Cover and chill 1 hour.

Roll out the dough on a lightly floured surface until it is ¾ inch thick. Cut the doughnuts and set aside.

Fill a pan or deep fryer about halfway with vegetable shortening and turn on medium heat. When the shortening is melted, at least 2 inches deep, and heated to 375 degrees F, you can start frying.

Cook doughnuts a few at a time until light golden brown. Turn and fry on the other side for 2 minutes. Remove to a tray lined with paper towels.

Place sugar and cinnamon in a small jar. Cover tightly and shake until well combined. Pour sugar mixture into a bowl or paper bag and toss warm doughnuts in the sugar mixture.

Packed in a sealed container, these doughnuts keep for up to a month in the freezer.

Maple Bread Pudding

This bread pudding is like a combination of custard and French toast. Breakfast and dessert at the same time. Yum! It pairs well with Winterport Winery's Winter Gold ice wine (see appendix).

Serves 6

¾ c plus ¼ c Maine maple syrup
2 t fresh lemon juice
2 T butter at room temperature
6 slices bread, with or without crusts (baguette, crusty bread, or cinnamon raisin bread)
4 eggs
2 egg yolks
2 c light cream
1 t cinnamon
½ t nutmeg
¼ t sea salt
2 t vanilla extract or rum
½ c currants, golden raisins, or dried cranberries

Preheat oven to 325 degrees F.

Grease a 3-quart baking dish. Pour in the syrup and lemon juice. Butter each slice of bread on one side and cut into ¾-inch cubes.

In a medium bowl, whisk together the eggs, egg yolks, cream, cinnamon, nutmeg, sea salt, and vanilla or rum. Add fruit and bread cubes and toss just until coated. Pour into baking dish. Bake 1 hour. The syrup will sink to the bottom and create a layer of thick maple goodness. Drizzle with another ¼ cup maple syrup and serve.

Chocolate Chèvre

Here is a different way to experience both chèvre (soft goat cheese) and chocolate. You can scoop the mixture into balls and serve with slices of tart apple and fresh berries. Whipped cream and a drizzle of melted chocolate on top finish the dish with flair. You can also use mascarpone or cream cheese as a substitute for the chévre.

Serves 12

12 oz dark or bittersweet chocolate bits
2 oz unsweetened baking chocolate, chopped
16 oz plain fresh chèvre
1 t vanilla extract
¼ t salt

Melt the chocolate bits and unsweetened chocolate together in a double boiler. Add the chèvre and stir until completely combined. Add vanilla and salt. Shape into balls or ovals or pipe into small dessert glasses. Serve with whipped cream.

Dark Chocolate Custard Pudding with Chantilly Cream

This chocolate custard is enhanced with mascarpone cheese. Intense and rich, it makes a wonderful end to a romantic dinner.

Makes 12 servings

2 c heavy cream
1 c whole milk
2½ c semisweet chocolate, finely chopped
½ c unsweetened baking chocolate, finely chopped
8 egg yolks
2 whole eggs
2 t vanilla extract
1 c (8 oz) mascarpone cheese
Chantilly Cream for topping

In the top of a double boiler, heat the cream, milk, semisweet chocolate, and unsweetened chocolate until melted, uniform in color, and hot.

In a large bowl, whisk the egg yolks and whole eggs until light and fluffy. Whisk 1 cup of the hot chocolate mixture into the eggs. Whisking constantly, pour the eggs back into the double boiler. Continue whisking until the mixture is very thick, smooth, and warm. Use caution: Overcooking the eggs will cause them to curdle.

Add the vanilla and mascarpone cheese. Stir until smooth and the cheese has been completely incorporated.

Pour into 12 individual dessert cups or a bowl, cover, and chill. Serve with fresh Chantilly Cream (page 44).

Chocolate Sea Moss Pudding

Sea moss, or Irish moss, is a sea vegetable that contains a lot of carrageenan, an ingredient used to thicken and stabilize milk products. (Just check the label on your ice cream.) It can thicken from twenty to two hundred times its weight in liquid. In traditional Maine cookery, it was used to thicken puddings. Give it a try—it will surprise you. Maine Coast Sea Vegetables harvests Irish moss and other sea vegetables (see appendix).

Makes 4 half-cup servings

½ c sugar
1 oz (1 square) unsweetened or bittersweet
   chocolate, finely chopped
4 T boiling water
2 c milk
handful (¼ c) dry sea moss

In a medium size, heavy-bottomed saucepan, combine the sugar, chopped chocolate, and boiling water. Heat, stirring constantly, for 2 minutes.

In a separate pan, slowly heat the milk. Wash the sea moss and put it into the milk. Heat the milk until bubbles form around the edge of the pan. Pour the chocolate mixture into the milk. Cook the pudding for 20 minutes, stirring all the while.

Pour the pudding through a fine mesh strainer into a medium bowl. Discard the solids. Whip the pudding for two minutes. Cover and chill. Serve with whipped cream or hot fudge.

Irish Moss

Strawberry Lemon Shortcake

Lemon butter spread on the warm shortcake biscuits gives this classic treat an extra layer of flavor.

Serves 6

Berries:
6 cups sliced fresh strawberries
¾ c sugar

Shortcake biscuits:
1 c flour
1 T sugar
1½ t baking powder
¼ t salt
⅓ c butter
1 egg yolk
¼ c milk
1 t finely grated lemon zest

Lemon butter:
4 T butter at room temperature
juice of 1 lemon
zest of 1 lemon
2 t sugar

Whipped cream:
1 c heavy cream
1 T sugar
1 t vanilla extract

Preheat oven to 450 degrees F.

In a medium bowl, combine the strawberries with ½ cup sugar. Mash slightly and stir to combine. Cover and chill.

In another medium bowl, combine the flour, sugar, baking powder, and salt. Stir. Cut in the butter until the mixture resembles coarse crumbs. In another bowl, whisk together the egg yolk, milk, and zest, and pour immediately into flour mixture. Stir with as few strokes as possible, until the mixture is just moist. Turn out onto a lightly floured surface and knead 2 minutes. Gently pat into a circle ¾-inch thick.

Cut into 6 pie-shaped pieces. Place pieces 2 inches apart on an ungreased baking sheet. Bake 8 to 10 minutes or until lightly brown. Remove from oven.

While shortcakes are baking, make the lemon butter: Stir together the butter, lemon juice, lemon zest, and sugar until completely combined.

When the shortcakes are done and cooled enough to handle, split biscuits in half horizontally and spread a thin layer of lemon butter on each half.

Whip the heavy cream until soft peaks form.

Sprinkle in the sugar, add the vanilla, and whip until firm peaks form.

To serve, place the bottom halves of the shortcakes on six individual plates. Spoon ½ cup of strawberries and juice over each shortcake. Top with a small dollop of whipped cream. Place the top half of each shortcake atop the cream. Spoon another ½-cup or so of berries over the tops of each. Finish with a flourish of whipped cream.

Blueberry Clafouti

Clafouti is a custard that makes its own "crust." First, a thin layer of the custard is baked in the pan, then the rest of the custard is added. The first layer becomes a crustlike base. You can substitute your favorite other fruit, but for a Maine touch use blueberries.

One 9-inch clafouti, serves 8 to10

4 eggs
1 c sugar
2 t vanilla extract
⅓ c all-purpose flour
½ t salt
¾ c Homemade Crème Fraîche (page 94)
   or sour cream
1¼ c heavy cream
16 oz fresh or frozen blueberries
2 T confectioners' sugar for sprinkling

Preheat oven to 350 degrees F.

Whisk together the eggs and sugar. Add the vanilla, flour, and salt. Whisk until completely combined. Gently stir in the crème fraîche and heavy cream. Grease a 9-inch deep-dish pie plate. Pour one third of the batter into the pan. Bake for five minutes or just until the batter is set.

Remove the pan from the oven and spread the blueberries evenly over the partially baked "crust." Pour the remaining batter gently over the blueberries. Return the pan to the oven and continue baking for 20 to 25 minutes or until the custard is done. The tip of a knife inserted into the center will come out clean. Cool on a wire rack. Chill at least 2 hours or overnight.

Sprinkle with confectioners' sugar before serving, or, to create a crème brûlée-style dessert, sprinkle a ⅛-inch layer of granulated sugar on top and caramelize it with a kitchen torch.

Cranberry Fluff

Cranberry fluff is the most amazing, luscious holiday dish. Yes, it uses mini marshmallows and, yes, I usually steer away from dishes that contain them. However, cranberry fluff is my exception. The marshmallows melt a bit to add their sweetness to the mixture. The cream lightens the texture and color, making this pink concoction just like a cloud in the sunrise. It's going to be a good day!

Serves 6 to 8

2 (12 oz) bags fresh cranberries
1½ c sugar
¼ t salt
⅛ t ground cayenne pepper
1 (10 oz) bag mini marshmallows
2 c heavy cream
5 c diced apples, peeled or unpeeled
¾ c chopped nuts (optional)

In a food processor, chop the cranberries until they are a fine, uniform consistency. Place the chopped berries in a bowl and add the sugar, salt, and cayenne pepper. Mix in the mini marshmallows. Cover and chill overnight.

Whip the cream until stiff peaks form. Stir the apples and nuts into the cranberry mixture. Fold the whipped cream into the berries and serve immediately. (This will keep overnight, but stir well before serving.)

Warm Berries with Dark Chocolate Truffle Sauce and Raspberry Coulis

You can serve this alone or pile the whole thing atop a scoop of vanilla ice cream. This treat pairs well with Coffee By Design's Brazil Monte Carmelo (see appendix).

Serves 6 to 8

Warm berries:
- 1 qt strawberries
- 1 qt Maine blueberries
- 1 qt raspberries
- 1 c Wyman's blueberry juice (see appendix)
- 1 T cornstarch
- 1 T cold water
- 1 c sifted confectioners' sugar

Chocolate truffle sauce:
- 12 oz semisweet chocolate bits
- 1 oz unsweetened chocolate
- 1/2 c heavy cream

Raspberry coulis:
- 1 qt raspberries
- ½ c confectioners' sugar, sifted

Wash and hull the strawberries. Wash the blueberries and raspberries. Set aside.

In a medium saucepan, heat the blueberry juice.

Dissolve the cornstarch in 1 tablespoon of cold water and add to the juice. Bring mixture to a boil. When it begins to thicken, stir in the confectioners' sugar. Add the strawberries, blueberries, and raspberries. Stir gently. Reduce heat and let the berries warm in the hot sauce for five minutes.

Place the semisweet and unsweetened chocolates and heavy cream in a small saucepan. Heat slowly, stirring constantly, until the chocolate is melted. Remove from heat.

In the bowl of a food processor, process the raspberries for the coulis, until they are puréed. Add the confectioners' sugar and process until it is completely liquefied. Strain the purée through a sieve into a clean bowl, stirring the mixture around to allow the juice to run through. Be sure to swipe the underside of the strainer with a rubber scraper or spoon to get all the juice.

Serve the berries in individual bowls. Spoon a generous dollop of chocolate sauce on top. Drape the chocolate with the raspberry coulis.

Harvest Pumpkin Flan with Maple Chantilly Cream

This flan is creamy and thick. You can even whip in 8 ounces of silken tofu for an additional protein kick and no one will know it is healthy. Sucanat is non-refined cane sugar. It is a dark brown color because it contains molasses.

Makes two 9-inch pies or a dozen 1-cup ramekins

8 eggs
3 T molasses
1/2 c Sucanat
1 t cinnamon
¼ t sea salt
½ t ground nutmeg
1 t fresh grated ginger root
2 T cornstarch
2 T water
1½ cups soy milk
2 c puréed cooked pumpkin
crystallized ginger for garnish

Preheat oven to 400 degrees F.

Grease two 9-inch pie plates or a dozen 1-cup ramekins. In the bowl of an electric mixer, whip eggs for 5 minutes until tripled in volume. Add molasses, Sucanat, cinnamon, sea salt, nutmeg, and grated ginger. Dissolve cornstarch in water and stir into soy milk. Add soy milk and pumpkin to egg mixture. Stir until well blended.

Divide equally between pie plates or ramekins. Bake at 400 degrees for 15 minutes. Turn oven down to 350 degrees. Bake pies for additional 35 minutes, ramekins for 15 minutes, or until a knife inserted in the center comes out clean.

Serve hot or cold with a dollop of Maple Chantilly Cream. Garnish with a piece of crystallized ginger.

Maple Chantilly Cream:
1 c heavy cream
3 T Maine maple syrup
1 t vanilla extract
⅛ t sea salt

Place cream in the bowl of an electric mixer. Whip until soft peaks form. Add remaining ingredients and whip until stiff peaks form. Chill.

Vanilla Cream Cheese Mousse Parfait with Fresh Strawberries

This parfait will delight your guests, and only you will know how easy and fast it is to make. It pairs well with Winterport Winery's Strawberry Wine.

Serves 6

8 oz cream cheese at room temperature
1¼ c sifted confectioners' sugar, divided
1 c chilled heavy cream
2 T vanilla extract
1 qt fresh strawberries

Using an electric mixer, whip the cream cheese until light and fluffy, about 5 minutes. Scrape the bowl down often to be sure there are no lumps. Slowly add ½ cup of the sifted confectioners' sugar.

In another bowl, beat the heavy cream. When soft peaks form, slowly add the vanilla and ½ cup of the sifted confectioners' sugar. Whip to stiff peaks.

Gently fold one third of the whipped cream into the cream cheese mixture. When it is completely incorporated, fold in another third of the whipped cream. Repeat with the last third.

Wash, dry, hull, and quarter the strawberries, reserving a few whole for garnishing. Place the cut berries in a small bowl and toss with 2 T confectioners' sugar.

Using six pretty wine glasses or a pretty glass serving bowl, place a dollop of mousse in the bottom. Arrange a layer of sweetened berries on the mousse. Softly add a layer of mousse on top of the berries. Repeat layering, ending with a layer of mousse on top.

Garnish with whole strawberries. Chill until ready to serve.

Berry Fool

Fruit fools are a combination of fruit and whipped cream. Strawberries, cranberries, and raspberries make this dish a pink burst of goodness. Blackberries and blueberries also work well. This dish pairs well with Cellardoor Vineyard's Sweetheart wine (see appendix).

Serves 4 to 6

1 pint (2 c) fresh berries, washed and free
   of stems and leaves
2 T water
½ c sugar
1 pint (2 c) heavy cream
1 T vanilla extract

Place the berries in a medium saucepan and stir in water and sugar. Cook over medium heat, stirring occasionally, for 10 minutes or until the berries are soft and have released their juices. Taste carefully and add more sugar to your liking. Remove from heat and set aside to cool completely.

When berries are cool, whip cream until stiff peaks form. Stir in vanilla. Pour cooled berries into bowl with cream. Gently fold together. Chill 2 hours. Serve mounded in pretty glasses and topped with whipped cream.

ENHANCEMENTS

Here are tasty tidbits that enhance an already wonderful dessert. Sometimes a little sauce or crunch on top is just what you need to make the ending of your meal achieve perfection.

Hot Fudge Sauce

This fudge sauce is thick and smooth. If you need less, cut the recipe in half.

Makes 6 cups

4 oz unsweetened baking chocolate
3 lb (four 12-oz packages) semisweet
   chocolate bits
2 c heavy cream
½ c hot water
⅓ c brown sugar
½ c unsalted butter

Melt all ingredients together in a double boiler or a heavy-bottomed medium pan on low heat. Whisk until smooth and glossy. Serve warm over ice cream or your favorite cake. Keeps for one week in the refrigerator.

Cocoa Maple Syrup

Buttery and chocolaty, this syrup is fantastic on ice cream, waffles, and fresh fruit. It multiplies well, so make a big batch and give some away.

Makes 1 cup

¾ c Maine maple syrup
2 T unsweetened cocoa powder
2 T unsalted butter
pinch of sea salt

Pour syrup into a small heavy-bottomed saucepan. Heat over medium heat until boiling. Whisk in cocoa powder, butter, and salt. Simmer two minutes, stirring constantly. Serve warm. Keeps for one week in the refrigerator.

Fresh Fruit Coulis

This bright, wonderful sauce captures the essence of the fruit. You taste all of the flavor without the seeds and pulp.

Makes 2 cups

1 pint (2 c) fresh or frozen fruit
½ c sugar

In a small saucepan, stir together the fruit and sugar over medium heat until the sugar has completely dissolved and the fruit has broken down. Strain the fruit mixture through a sieve into a bowl, pressing on the pulp to extract all the juice. Discard the seeds and pulp.

Granola

Add a little crunch to your parfait. Spice up your ice cream. Sprinkle on your yogurt. Granola is easy to make and adaptable to your taste. Save a penny here and there by making it yourself. You may add or subtract ingredients, as long as you keep the overall proportion of wet ingredients to dry ingredients the same.

Makes 4 cups

2 c regular rolled oats
½ c toasted or raw wheat germ
½ c flaked coconut
2 T brown sugar
½ c honey or Maine maple syrup
⅓ c vegetable oil
1 t vanilla extract
¼ c flax seeds
¼ c sunflower seeds
¼ c chopped almonds
½ c dried cherries or currants

Preheat oven to 350 degrees F.

Toss all ingredients together in a large bowl. Spread in an even layer on a cookie sheet. Bake for 15 minutes. Remove from oven. Return hot granola to large bowl and stir until cool.

Cardinal Sauce

This recipe comes from a summer day. After picking strawberries by the bucketful...I met up with a friend who offered me some raspberries to go with them. We took the berries home and mixed up a batch of vanilla ice cream. We just knew that this batch of homemade ice cream was destined to be topped with our berries. I whipped up this sauce to go on top.

Makes about 5 cups

2 c water
4 T cornstarch
1/2 c sugar, or to taste
1 quart fresh (or 16 oz frozen) strawberries, hulled and mashed
1 quart fresh (or 16 oz frozen) raspberries, mashed

For variations, add one of the following:
juice and zest of one lime or lemon
2 T orange juice concentrate
1 t cinnamon or nutmeg

Place water, cornstarch, and sugar in a medium saucepan and stir until smooth. Stir over medium heat until boiling. When it begins to thicken, add strawberries and raspberries. Stir to coat. Continue stirring until thick and bright. Taste carefully and add more sugar if needed.

If you have Cardinal Sauce left over, you can cool it completely and fold it into an equal amount of stiffly whipped cream. This creates a beautiful, light berry mousse—a wonderful end to a summer meal.

Brown Sugar Spiced Pepitas

Crunchy with a zip-tang, these pumpkin seeds are great as a garnish or by the handful. They're addictive!

Makes 1 cup

1 T vegetable oil
1 c (¼ lb) pepitas, raw (green, not toasted)
½ t salt
⅛ t cayenne pepper
1 T light brown sugar

In a 12-inch heavy-bottomed pan, warm the oil over medium-low heat. Add the pepitas and stir constantly until the seeds are golden and puffed, about 8 to 10 minutes. Remove the pepitas with a slotted spoon and place in a bowl. Sprinkle with salt, cayenne, and brown sugar. Toss gently until coated.

Maple Mascarpone Cream

Wonderful on fruit desserts, this cream is thick and scrumptious.

Makes 1 cup

1 c (8 oz) mascarpone cheese
2 generous T Maine maple syrup
1 T fresh lemon juice

Gently whisk the mascarpone cheese in a small bowl until it is a creamy consistency. Add the syrup and lemon juice. Whisk until completely combined. Chill until ready to use. You can make this a day ahead but be sure to whisk it just a bit before using.

Homemade Crème Fraîche

Use on a slice of warm cake for a tangy, rich sensation. You need the pasteurized (not ultra-pasteurized) cream to work effectively with the buttermilk or sour cream to thicken the crème fraîche properly.

Makes 2 cups

2 c organic pasteurized (not ultra-pasteurized)
 cream
2 T cultured buttermilk or sour cream

Whisk together the cream and buttermilk. Pour into a clean glass jar, cover, and let stand at room temperature for 8 to 24 hours, until thick. Store refrigerated for up to 10 days.

Blood Orange Curd

Blood oranges are in season for only a short time during winter, but they are gorgeous and deserve whatever attention we can give them when they arrive. This luscious pink-tinged curd is delicious on angel food cake.

Makes about 3 cups

4 blood oranges
6 egg yolks
½ c unsalted butter
1 c sugar

Wash the oranges. Zest them and then juice them. In a small bowl, whisk half the juice into the egg yolks.

Place the other half of the juice, zest, butter, and sugar into a heavy-bottomed saucepan on low heat. Whisk constantly until the sugar is dissolved. Remove from heat. Add ½ cup of the hot mixture to the eggs, whisking constantly. Return the warmed eggs to the pan, whisking constantly. Heat this mixture gently until thick, but do not boil or it will separate.

Strain mixture through a fine mesh sieve. Pour into a clean, hot jar. Cover and chill until ready to use.

Butterscotch Caramel Sauce

T his is the real deal. Pack it in pretty jars and give it as a gift—your friends will thank you, just as I thank my friend Linda who gave me a version of the recipe. It's wonderful over ice cream or apple crisp.

Makes 5 cups

½ c water
2 c sugar
12 T (1½ sticks) plus 2 T unsalted butter
1 c sweetened condensed milk
2 c heavy cream
1 T vanilla extract

Place water and sugar in a heavy-bottomed medium saucepan and bring to a boil without stirring. Using a silicone or bristle pastry brush dipped in hot water, wash down any sugar crystals that form on the side of the pan. Cook, without stirring, 10 minutes or just until syrup turns a deep golden color. Reduce the heat to low and whisk in 12 tablespoons butter, a tablespoon at a time. Whisk in the sweetened condensed milk and heavy cream. Gradually bring to a boil, whisking constantly until thickened, another 4 minutes. Stir in the vanilla.

Remove from heat. In a small heavy-bottomed pan, heat 2 tablespoons butter until it becomes lightly browned. Remove from heat and stir into the sauce. Serve warm.

Candied Citrus Peel

Although these recipe directions call for lemon peel, grapefruit, lime, and orange work equally well. The candied peel makes a great addition to fruitcake and a perfect garnish for dishes containing citrus. You can also enjoy it just as it is for a special sweet-tart snack.

Makes ¾ cup

4 lemons
4 c plus 1 c water
1 c plus ½ c sugar

Remove the zest from the lemons in wide strips with a vegetable peeler. Be sure to take off only the colored part of the rind and leave the white pith behind. Cut the pieces lengthwise with a sharp knife into ⅛-inch-wide strips. Reserve lemons for juicing.

Fill a 2-quart heavy-bottomed saucepan with 4 cups of water. Add sliced peel. Bring to a boil. Reduce heat and simmer 15 minutes. Drain in a fine mesh sieve and rinse well.

Bring 1 cup water and 1 cup sugar to a boil in the saucepan, stirring until sugar has dissolved. Add peel and gently simmer until translucent, about 15 minutes.

Remove peel from syrup with a slotted spoon, letting syrup drain off into saucepan.

Spread peel on a sheet of parchment paper and cool to room temperature. Toss the cooked peel with ½ cup sugar, stirring with a fork to coat and separate. Place sugared peel in a clean dry sieve and shake off extra sugar. Spread individual pieces out on a fresh sheet of parchment paper to dry slightly. Store in an airtight container in the freezer until ready to use.

Blackberry Syrup

This syrup is sweet and full of fruit flavor. Substitute other berries to create a series of syrups to top desserts or pancakes.

Makes 4 cups

1½ c sugar
1 c water
2 c blackberries, fresh or frozen

In a small saucepan, combine sugar, water, and blackberries. Bring to a boil over medium-high heat, stirring occasionally. When mixture boils, reduce heat to medium-low and simmer 5 minutes, stirring occasionally, until sugar is completely dissolved.

Remove pan from heat and cool for 15 minutes. Strain syrup through a fine mesh sieve into a clean glass jar or other sealable container. Chill. Store covered in the refrigerator for up to 7 days.

Fresh Blueberry Sauce

This thick sweet sauce captures the sweet, summery flavor of Maine blueberries.

Makes 4 cups

2 T sugar
1 T cornstarch
1 c cold water
3 c Maine blueberries, fresh or frozen
1 T lemon zest
2 T fresh lemon juice

In a small saucepan, combine sugar and cornstarch. Gradually stir in water. Cook over medium heat, stirring constantly, until mixture comes to a boil and is slightly thickened and clear. Gently stir in blueberries, lemon zest, and lemon juice. Once the berries are coated, use immediately or chill for later. Serve warm or chilled.

CANDY

Candy is a sweet reward. A little goes a long way. Though filled with sugary goodness, it is not the enemy as long as we can take just one. A simple, lovely dessert is a plate of candies, one per person or a small assortment to tempt the taste buds. All types can be stored in the freezer in an airtight container.

Maine Needhams

Mashed potato and coconut are the base for these favorite Maine confections. If you like to make special gifts for family and friends, Needhams are perfect. They are dense and moist, reminiscent of macaroons. Adding paraffin to the chocolate yields a firmer, longer lasting coating.

Makes 24 candies

1 c warm mashed Maine potatoes (completely unseasoned)
½ c unsalted butter
2 lb confectioners' sugar
8 oz flaked coconut
2 t vanilla extract
½ t salt
chocolate for dipping
paraffin (optional; see note below)

Combine all the ingredients in a bowl and mix well. Line a 9 by 13-inch pan with plastic wrap and grease the plastic lightly with butter. Press the mixture evenly into the lined pan. Cover and chill until firm.

Uncover the candies and remove from the pan.

Peel off the plastic wrap and cut the firmed filling into 24 squares.

NOTE: If you plan to serve the candies within two days, you can leave out the paraffin. If you are going to give them as gifts and want to be sure they stay fresh longer, include the paraffin to make a firmer chocolate shell.

Dipping Chocolate:

12 oz semisweet chocolate chips
4 oz (4 squares) finely chopped unsweetened chocolate
½ cake (2½ inches square) paraffin wax, grated or chopped finely. (The kind used for sealing jelly jars, found in the baking aisle of your grocery store.)

Melt the paraffin in a double boiler. Add the chocolates. Stir constantly until the wax and chocolates are melted and smooth. Remove from heat.

A toothpick or cake tester may be used to dip the Needham squares. Dip each square of filling until it is completed enrobed in the chocolate. Hold the square above the chocolate mixture after dipping so any excess chocolate drips back into the double boiler. Place on waxed paper to harden. If the chocolate begins to stiffen in the double boiler, return to low heat until the chocolate becomes liquid enough for dipping.

Maple Peanut Brittle

This is a super-secret recipe that comes out great every time. I'll keep the secret of where it came from. You make it for your family and friends and enjoy their peanutty smiles.

Makes 4 cups

½ c light corn syrup
½ c Maine maple syrup
1 c sugar
¼ c water
2 T corn oil margarine
1¾ c roasted peanuts, salted or unsalted
1 t baking soda

Line two 11 by 17-inch baking sheets with parchment or silicone mats.

In a large saucepan, stir the corn syrup, maple syrup, sugar, water, and margarine until boiling: 200 degrees F on a candy thermometer. Stop stirring and cook until the mixture reaches 280 degrees F. Using a silicone or soft bristle brush dipped in hot water, wash down any crystals that form on the sides of the pan.

Gradually stir in peanuts. Continue cooking until the thermometer reads 305 degrees F about 5 minutes. Stir in baking soda. Cook, stirring for 5 minutes more.

Pour half of the mixture onto each of the lined baking sheets. Spread out to ¼ inch thick. Cool completely.

Maple Almond Toffee

Toffee is great placed in pretty boxes lined with wax paper as a holiday gift. The maple scent and flavor are delectable.
Makes 4 cups

1 c unsalted butter
1 c sugar
¼ c Maine maple syrup
1 c chopped blanched almonds
1 c semisweet or milk chocolate bits

In a heavy-bottomed 3-quart saucepan, melt butter. Add sugar and maple syrup. Turn heat to high and stir rapidly until the color changes to light amber, about 4 minutes. Add nuts. Continue stirring until almonds start to pop. Mixture will have a compact appearance but still be fluid enough to pour. Be sure the sugar is melted and caramel-colored, but be careful: this mixture burns easily.

Remove from heat and pour onto an ungreased 9 by 13-inch pan. Spread as thin as possible. Sprinkle with chocolate bits. Let sit for 3 minutes until they start to melt and lose their shape, then spread the chocolate evenly over the toffee. Cool. Break into pieces and store in an airtight container.

Maple Cream Candies

Just like the maple sugar candies you find in tourist shops around Maine, these sweet delights are perfect tiny treats for giving.
Makes several dozen, depending on size

1 c maple sugar
1 c brown sugar
¼ c water
¼ t vanilla extract
walnut or other nutmeats (optional)

In a small heavy-bottomed saucepan, cook maple sugar, brown sugar, and water until they reach 240 degrees F (soft-ball stage) on a candy thermometer. Add vanilla. Remove from heat and cool to room temperature. Beat vigorously until creamy and slightly firm.

Knead on a cold, smooth surface until smooth. (I use a marble slab.) Scoop with a tiny ice cream scoop or use a teaspoon and form into small balls, about 1 teaspoon each. Press a nutmeat on top of each if you like. Store in an airtight container when completely cool.

Dark Chocolate Fudge

This is the best fudge recipe I've found, bar none. It comes out great every time. Be absolutely sure to set the timer when the mixture comes to a true boil, and stir away until it dings. Add nuts, dried fruit, mini marshmallows, or chopped candy canes at your discretion. For a white chocolate version, substitute white chocolate for the semisweet bits and omit the unsweetened baking chocolate.

Makes about 5 pounds

5 c sugar
2 small (5 oz) cans evaporated milk
½ c (1 stick) butter
16 oz Marshmallow Fluff
1 t salt
4 oz unsweetened baking chocolate, finely chopped
24 oz semisweet chocolate bits
2 t vanilla extract
1 c nuts (optional)

Grease two 9 by 13-inch pans. Line the pans with foil and grease it as well.

Combine the sugar, evaporated milk, butter, Marshmallow Fluff, and salt in a large saucepan. Stirring constantly, melt the ingredients together over low heat. Stir all the way down to the bottom of the pan, scraping the entire surface. As sugars begin to caramelize they can burn easily.

Raise the heat to medium and bring the mixture to a boil. Make sure it is a true boil, not just air bubbles escaping as you stir. Set the timer as soon as you see the first real boiling bubble. Boil, stirring constantly, for 6 minutes. Remove from heat.

Add unsweetened chocolate, chocolate bits, vanilla, and nuts. Stir until chocolate is melted and incorporated. Pour immediately into the baking pans and quickly spread evenly with a metal spatula. Cool.

Slice cooled fudge into 1-inch squares or desired size. When completely cool, remove from pan and store in an airtight container.

Fried Truffles

Can you imagine deep, dark chocolate, coated in a crispy crust, cooked golden brown with a molten core? This is a special-occasion dessert. It's hard to eat just one, so invite lots of friends over to share.
Makes 3 dozen

1 c heavy cream
1 lb semisweet chocolate, finely chopped
2 oz unsweetened baking chocolate, finely chopped
10 oz stale French bread (half a baguette)
¼ c sugar
1 T cinnamon
⅛ t cayenne pepper (optional)
¾ c flour
4 eggs, beaten
vegetable shortening for frying

Heat the cream in a small heavy-bottomed saucepan until bubbles form around the edge of the pan. Slowly mix in the semisweet and unsweetened chocolates, stirring constantly until the mixture is smooth and satiny.

Pour into a bowl, cover, and place in the freezer. Give it a stir every twenty minutes for about three hours. You want to end up with a thick claylike ganache.

Line a baking pan with parchment paper. Scoop out pieces of ganache, roll into ¾-inch balls, and place them on the parchment. Freeze for 45 minutes.

Use a food processor to pulse the bread into very fine crumbs. Add the sugar, cinnamon, and cayenne, and pulse again.

Set three shallow bowls on your counter. From left to right, you want flour, eggs, and about a cup of the breadcrumb-sugar mixture. (Don't put all the breadcrumbs in at once as they will get clumpy from the eggs.) Using your left hand, take a ball of the ganache and roll it in the flour, then drop it into the egg mixture. With your right hand, coat the ball well with egg, let it drip off a bit, and transfer it to the breadcrumbs. Coat well and place it on your baking pan.

After all the ganache balls have been coated, repeat the process one more time: flour, egg, breadcrumbs. At the end of the second breading, the truffles should be almost the size of a golf ball.

Place back in the freezer for two hours or overnight. They can be frozen at this point in an airtight container. Be sure to layer them with plastic wrap or parchment paper. If they touch while they're freezing, they will stick together.

When you are ready to cook the truffles, line a tray with brown paper or paper towels in several layers. Put shortening into your fryer and bring it to 375 degrees F. Fry two truffles at a time, watching them carefully. Cook them until they are golden brown, about a minute. Remove to the tray to drain. Serve hot. OMG!

Specialty Products from Maine Producers

Appleton Creamery

780 Gurneytown Road, Appleton, ME 04862
www.appletoncreamery.com

This creamery's award-winning chèvre comes in a variety of flavors and sizes.

Bakewell Cream

New England Cupboard / Winterport Company
54 Perry Road, Bangor, ME 04401
(207) 941-1152
www.newenglandcupboard.com

"A superior leavening agent famous for its no-fail tall, light, and flaky biscuits."

Bartlett Maine Estate Winery

West Bay Road (Me. Rte. 186), Gouldsboro, ME 04607
(207) 546-2408
www.bartlettwinery.com

"We're committed to using only pure, top quality fruits that grow naturally in our region."

Cellardoor Vineyard

367 Youngtown Road, Lincolnville, ME 04849
(207) 763-4478
www.mainewine.com

"Beautiful wines grown and created on the coast of Maine."

Coffee By Design

43 Washington Avenue, Portland, ME 04101
(207) 879-2233
www.coffeebydesign.com

"Our mission is to educate people about specialty coffee and provide the best beans available."

Coastline Confections and Nutmeg Foods

175 Main Street, South Portland, ME 04106
(207) 239-7001
www.nutmegfoods.com

"Coastline uses fresh local ingredients to support the local economy and produce the most delicious chocolate possible."

Dean's Sweets

82 Middle Street, Portland, ME 04101
(207) 899-3664
www.deanssweets.com

"Nut-free chocolates made with fresh local ingredients."

Goranson Farm

250 River Road, Dresden, ME 04342
(207) 737-8834
http://home.gwi.net/~goransonfarm/index.htm

Certified organic berry and vegetable farm with on-farm market.

Maine Coast Sea Vegetables, Inc.

3 George's Pond Road, Franklin, ME 04634
(207) 565-2907
www.seaveg.com

Source for Irish moss flakes for making custard.

Maine Gold Maple Syrup and Gifts

229 Park Street, Rockland, ME 04841
(800) 752-5271 or 207-593-0090
www.mainegold.com

"100 percent pure, award-winning maple syrup."

Maine Sea Salt Company

11 Church Lane, Marshfield, ME 04654

(207) 255-3310

www.maineseasalt.com

"The first salt works in Maine in over 200 years."

North Star Orchards

97 Orchard Road, Madison, ME 04950

(207) 696-5109 or (877) 696-5109

northstarorchards@tds.net

"Apple jams, jellies, and preserves from local Macintosh Farm. Numerous varieties of apples available."

Quoddy Mist

72 Water Street, Lubec, ME 04652

(207) 733-4847

www.quoddymist.com

"All-natural high-quality sea salt in a variety of grades, crystal sizes, and flavors."

Pastor Chuck Orchards

(207) 773-1314

www.pastorchuckorchards.com

Delicious organic apple butter, applesauce, and salsas.

Rising Tide Community Market

15 Coastal Market Place, Damariscotta, ME 04543

(207) 563-5556

www.risingtide.coop

"A member-owned natural foods cooperative committed to providing local, natural and organic food."

State of Maine Cheese Company

461 Commercial Street, Rockport, ME 04856

(800) 762-8895 or (207) 236-8895

www.cheese-me.com

"Our cheese is all-natural or certified organic and made with the best milk attainable."

Stonewall Kitchen

2 Stonewall Lane, York, ME 03909

(207) 351-2713

www.stonewallkitchen.com

Jams and preserves, mustards, chutneys, sauces and salsas, dessert toppings, and baking kits

Sweetgrass Farm Winery and Distillery

347 Carroll Road, Union, ME 04862

(207) 785-3024

www.sweetgrasswinery.com

"Maine's first winery and distillery using Maine grown fruit: apple, cranberry apple, blueberry, and peach."

Wilbur's of Maine Chocolate Confections

32 Independence Drive, Freeport, ME 04032

(207) 865-4071

www.wilburs.com

"A full line of quality chocolate, from blueberry cream to chocolate-covered wild Maine blueberry truffles."

Winterport Winery / Penobscot Bay Brewery

279 South Main Street, Winterport, ME 04496

(207) 223-4500

www.winterportwinery.com

Award-winning wines and beers made with local ingredients.

Jasper Wyman and Son Blueberry Products

Milbridge, ME 04568

(207) 546-2311

www.wymans.com

tom@wymans.com

Frozen berries, canned berries, and juice— available at most grocers or direct from Wyman's.

Recipe Index